Frommer's®

W9-CAB-918

London
day BY day

1st Edition

by Lesley Logan

WILEY
Wiley Publishing, Inc.

Contents

Published by:

Wiley Publishing, Inc.

111 River St.
Hoboken, NJ 07030-5774

ISBN-13: 978-0-7645-7618-8
ISBN-10: 0-7645-7618-6

Editor: Naomi P. Kraus
Production Editor: M. Faunette Johnston
Photo Editor: Richard Fox
Cartographer: Nicholas Trotter
Savvy Traveler illustrations by Rashell Smith and Karl Brandt
Production by Wiley Indianapolis Composition Services

For information on our other products and services or to obtain technical
support, please contact our Customer Care Department within the U.S.
at 800/762-2974, outside the U.S. at 317/572-3993 or fax 317/572-4002.

Wiley also publishes its books in a variety of electronic formats. Some
content that appears in print may not be available in electronic formats.

Manufactured in China

5   4   3

A Note from the Publisher

Organizing your time. That's what this guide is all about.

Other guides give you long lists of things to see and do and then expect you to fit the pieces together. The Day by Day guides are different. These guides tell you the best of everything, and then they show you how to see it *in the smartest, most time-efficient way*. Our authors have designed detailed itineraries organized by time, neighborhood, or special interest. And each tour comes with a bulleted map that takes you from stop to stop.

Hoping to relive the glory days of Merrie Olde England, or to tour the highlights of the British Museum? Planning a walk through Chelsea, or a whirlwind tour of the very best that London has to offer? Whatever your interest or schedule, the Day by Days give you the smartest route to follow. Not only do we take you to the top sights and attractions, but we introduce you to those special moments that only locals know about—those "finds" that turn tourists into travelers.

The Day by Days are also your top choice if you're looking for one complete guide for all your travel needs. The best hotels and restaurants for every budget, the greatest shopping values, the wildest nightlife—it's all here.

Why should you trust our judgment? Because our authors personally visit each place they write about. They're an independent lot who say what they think and would never include places they wouldn't recommend to their best friends. They're also open to suggestions from readers. If you'd like to contact them, please send your comments my way at mspring@wiley.com, and I'll pass them on.

Enjoy your Day by Day guide—the most helpful travel companion you can buy. And have the trip of a lifetime.

Warm regards,

Michael Spring, Publisher
Frommer's Travel Guides

About the Author

Lesley Logan, a freelance travel writer and editor, is an American expatriate who has lived in London for over a decade. She's written several travel guidebooks, including *The Unofficial Guide to London*, and the *Berlitz Pocket Guide to London*. She is currently working on the new edition of *The Florman Guide to Europe's Best Restaurants*.

Acknowledgements

I'd like to thank my brilliant editor, Naomi Kraus, for her unflagging energy, extensive knowledge of London, and exquisite eye for details; she was very generous in every way, going far beyond the call of duty in creating this book. I am also grateful for the assistance of Emma Littlewood and Rebecca Tetley in researching this book. Thanks also to Antonella and everyone at the cafe, for great food and London insights. Lastly, my deepest gratitude to my husband Tom and daughter Nora, who make London home for me.

An Additional Note

Please be advised that travel information is subject to change at any time—and this is especially true of prices. We therefore suggest that you write or call ahead for confirmation when making your travel plans. The authors, editors, and publisher cannot be held responsible for the experiences of readers while traveling. Your safety is important to us, however, so we encourage you to stay alert and be aware of your surroundings.

Star Ratings, Icons & Abbreviations

Every hotel, restaurant, and attraction listing in this guide has been ranked for quality, value, service, amenities, and special features using a **star-rating system.** Hotels, restaurants, attractions, shopping, and nightlife are rated on a scale of zero stars (recommended) to three stars (exceptional). In addition to the star-rating system, we also use a **kids icon** to point out the best bets for families.

The following **abbreviations** are used for credit cards:

AE	American Express	DISC	Discover	V	Visa
DC	Diners Club	MC	MasterCard		

Frommers.com

Now that you have the guidebook to a great trip, visit our website at **www.frommers.com** for travel information on more than 3,000 destinations. With features updated regularly, we give you instant access to the most current trip-planning information available. At Frommers.com, you'll also find the best prices on airfares, accommodations, and car rentals—and you can even book travel online through our travel booking partners.

A Note on Prices

Frommer's provides exact prices in each destination's local currency. As this book went to press, the rate of exchange was £1 = US$1.93. Rates of exchange are constantly in flux; for up-to-the-minute information, consult a currency-conversion website such as www.oanda.com/convert/classic.

In the Take a Break and Best Bets section of this book, we have used a system of dollar signs to show a range of costs for one night in a hotel (the price of a double-occupancy room) or the cost of an entrée at a restaurant. Use the following table to decipher the dollar signs:

Cost	Hotels	Restaurants
$	under $150	under $20
$$	$150–$250	$20–$30
$$$	$250–$350	$30–$40
$$$$	$350–$450	$40–$50
$$$$$	over $450	over $50

An Invitation to the Reader

In researching this book, we discovered many wonderful places—hotels, restaurants, shops, and more. We're sure you'll find others. Please tell us about them, so we can share the information with your fellow travelers in upcoming editions. If you were disappointed with a recommendation, we'd love to know that, too. Please write to:

Frommer's London Day by Day, 1st Edition
Wiley Publishing, Inc. • 111 River St. • Hoboken, NJ 07030

16 Favorite
Moments

16 Favorite Moments

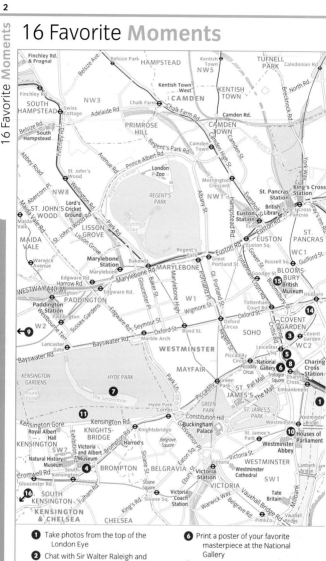

1. Take photos from the top of the London Eye

2. Chat with Sir Walter Raleigh and other historical figures at the Tower of London

3. Eat ice cream at the intermission of a first-class production

4. Drink champagne and dig the music (classical or jazz) at the Late View at the V&A

5. Dine next to a celebrity at the Ivy

6. Print a poster of your favorite masterpiece at the National Gallery

7. Crisscross the scenic Serpentine in a paddle boat

8. Finish a brass rubbing at St Martins-in-the-Field

9. Haggle for a bargain at Portobello Road Market

10. Listen to Big Ben strike the hour

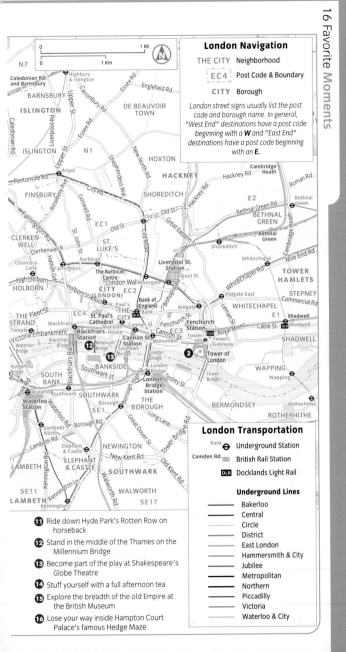

London Transportation

Bank ⊖   Underground Station

Camden Rd. ▦   British Rail Station

DLR   Docklands Light Rail

Underground Lines

——— Bakerloo
——— Central
········ Circle
——— District
——— East London
——— Hammersmith & City
——— Jubilee
——— Metropolitan
——— Northern
——— Piccadilly
——— Victoria
——— Waterloo & City

11 Ride down Hyde Park's Rotten Row on horseback

12 Stand in the middle of the Thames on the Millennium Bridge

13 Become part of the play at Shakespeare's Globe Theatre

14 Stuff yourself with a full afternoon tea

15 Explore the breadth of the old Empire at the British Museum

16 Lose your way inside Hampton Court Palace's famous Hedge Maze

"When a man is tired of London, he's tired of Life, for there is in London all that Life can afford." Dr. Samuel Johnson may have been exaggerating a bit, but boredom with London may indeed be a sign of depression. On the rare occasions I become weary of this marvelous city, the experiences outlined in this section are my mood-elevating prescriptions. Side effects may include euphoria, infatuation, and a sudden loss of pounds (sterling, that is).

1 Take photos from the top of the London Eye. The top of this Ferris wheel is the best place to get a picture-perfect shot of London's far-reaching landscape. Any time is a good time to take this "flight," but for a truly breathtaking photo op, jump aboard on a late afternoon as the sun starts sinking and the lights come on across the city. See p 12, bullet 7.

2 Chat with Sir Walter Raleigh, William the Conqueror, and other historical figures at the Tower of London. The Tower's entertaining actors have their characters' life stories down pat, and are walking, talking history. Don't be shy; they love to interact with visitors and answer questions. They may even approach you in a friendly manner as you wander around. See p 16, bullet 1.

3 Eat ice cream at the intermission of a first-class production as a well-deserved splurge for having gotten a half-price ticket for a very good seat at one of London's many famous theaters. If ice cream's not your thing, order drinks before your play starts, and pick them up during the "interval." See p 133.

4 Drink champagne and dig the music (classical or jazz) at the Late View at the V&A, held under the museum's thrilling Dale Chilhuly glass chandelier on Wednesdays and the last Friday of each month. Several of the renowned museum's galleries are open for exploring, and the relaxed atmosphere makes for a much more leisurely visit. Pick up a ticket for one of the lectures that start at 7pm, and round out the night with dinner at the candlelit cafe downstairs. See p 26.

5 Dine next to a celebrity at the Ivy, but act unimpressed. Don't even think about autographs, cameras, or

A pod on the British London Eye.

Holbein's The Ambassadors *is just one of many National Gallery masterpieces.*

gaping at this London glamour hot spot, where the modern British cuisine is good and the clientele stellar. Make your reservation a month in advance of your visit; weeknights are better than weekends for star-gazing, and remember that only Americans eat dinner before 8pm. *See p 102.*

6 Print a poster of your favorite masterpiece at the National Gallery. The computers in this world-renowned museum's Sainsbury Wing offer virtual reconnaissance tours of this huge, treasure-packed museum and let you print out high-quality posters of your favorite paintings in a variety of sizes. The database is huge and intelligently organized—it's a real kick to scroll through. *See p 22, bullet 7.*

7 Crisscross the scenic Serpentine in a paddle boat on a sunny morning as ducks and geese wheel overhead. The little island on the north side is reputed to be local resident J. M. Barrie's inspiration for the Island of the Lost Boys in *Peter Pan.* Bring a camera and your energy, or opt for a rowboat and let a companion do the work. *See p 88, bullet 5.*

8 Finish a brass rubbing at St. Martin-in-the-Fields, an activity perfect for one of London's many rainy afternoons. There are dozens of beautiful brasses of different sizes and styles to choose from. The finished work makes a perfect (and relatively inexpensive) souvenir. It's a big hit with kids. *See p 43, bullet 4.*

9 Haggle for a bargain at Portobello Road Market, either at the open-air stalls, or in the warrens of indoor arcades. You may get 10% to 15% off the asking price, which everyone involved knows is just set for that probability. Saturday's the best day to come to this antiques market, and even the seething crowds won't ruin the fun. *See p 82.*

10 Listen to Big Ben strike the hour, an event that thrills even Londoners. It's the bell itself that's named Big Ben, though most assign that name to the whole clock tower. Though the bell has a crack in it and can't sound an E note, its chimed aria from Handel's *Messiah* is the undisputed aural symbol of London. *See p 10, bullet 2.*

Outdoor stalls at Portobello Road Market.

Riders trot down Hyde Park's Rotten Row.

⑪ Ride down Hyde Park's Rotten Row on horseback and you'll feel like a character from a 19th-century English novel, as you pass joggers, in-line skaters, and bicyclists. There's no better way to absorb the atmosphere of London's most popular park. Only skilled riders should let their horses try a canter; novices will enjoy the experience most at a walking gait. *See p 87, bullet* ❸.

⑫ Stand in the middle of the Thames on the Millennium Bridge, which spans not just the river, but the centuries, with

A view of St. Paul's Cathedral from the Millenium Bridge.

St. Paul's Cathedral on one side and the Tate Modern on the other. The views of the cityscape are impressive, especially at sunrise and sunset. *See p 13, bullet* ❿.

⑬ Become part of the play at Shakespeare's Globe Theatre as one of the "groundlings" who stand in front of the stage, much as the rabble did during Shakespeare's time. You never know when the actors might mingle among you as they bellow out their lines. It's a truly Elizabethan experience, minus the thieves and the spitting. *See p 133.*

⑭ Stuff yourself with a full afternoon tea at one of the many luxe hotels that rise to the task of impressing visitors with an array of tea sandwiches, scones, clotted cream, and desserts—all washed down with a strong cuppa. Make no dinner plans—you won't need them. *See p 94.*

⑮ Explore the breadth of the old Empire at the British Museum, where priceless treasures acquired from all parts of the globe—including the Rosetta Stone and the Elgin Marbles—testify to the power that Britain once exerted over the farthest reaches of the world, and give you insight into just how greedy its adventurers were. If your interests tend more toward the literary, there are few better places in the world to soak up the power of the written word than the museum's famous Reading Room. *See p 30.*

⑯ Lose your way inside Hampton Court Palace's famous Hedge Maze, whose winding paths cover nearly half a mile. When you manage to extricate yourself from its clutches, stroll through the many centuries of architectural styles featured at this stunning palace, which was the home of many an English monarch. Don't neglect the gift shops. *See p 51, bullet* ❾. ●

The Best **in One Day**

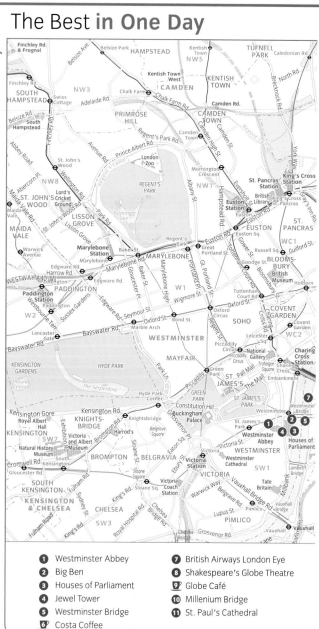

1. Westminster Abbey
2. Big Ben
3. Houses of Parliament
4. Jewel Tower
5. Westminster Bridge
6. Costa Coffee
7. British Airways London Eye
8. Shakespeare's Globe Theatre
9. Globe Café
10. Millenium Bridge
11. St. Paul's Cathedral

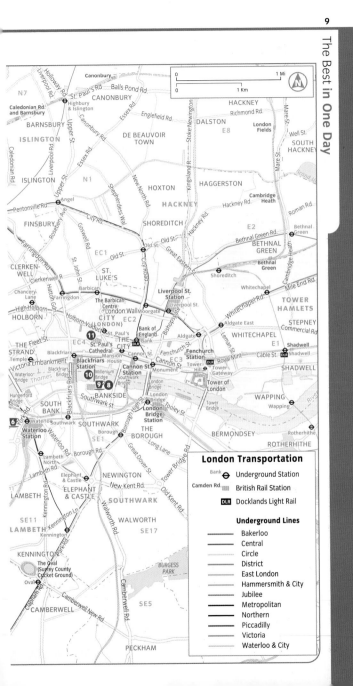

London Transportation

Underground Station

British Rail Station

Docklands Light Rail

Underground Lines

Bakerloo
Central
Circle
District
East London
Hammersmith & City
Jubilee
Metropolitan
Northern
Piccadilly
Victoria
Waterloo & City

With London's bounty of sights, how do you choose what to see in a day? In this tour, you'll see the oldest (Westminster Abbey); the newest (British Airways London Eye); and something that stands (time-wise) in between: the painstakingly authentic reconstruction of Shakespeare's Globe Theatre. Throw in beautiful vistas along the Thames River from some of the city's loveliest bridges, and you've got yourself a great one-day jaunt that won't leave you feeling exhausted. START: **Westminster Tube Station**

❶ ★★★ Westminster Abbey.

Westminster Abbey is one of the finest examples of medieval architecture in Europe. Laid to rest here are the towering figures of English life. Some 3,300 memorials to kings, nobles, and an assortment of church worthies are here for the viewing. William the Conqueror, Edward III (who willed that his heart be removed before burial to rest with his mum's remains in Grey Friar's Church), Mary Queen of Scots, Elizabeth I (whose death mask was the model for her tomb's figure), and Henry V, the hero of Agincourt—all have elaborately decorated sarcophagi. Don't miss the Gothic ceilings (reflected in a large mirror for viewing), the stained glass in the Chapter House, and the elaborate carvings of the Henry VIII Chapel's choir stalls. And make your

The Choir Apse at Westminster Abbey.

way to Poet's Corner, where you'll find monuments to well-loved literary names such as Chaucer, Austen, and Dickens. ⏱ 1½ hr. Arrive before 9:30am to avoid lines. 20 Dean's Yard. ☎ 0207/222-5152. www. westminster-abbey.org. Admission £7.50 adults, £5 seniors & kids 11–16, £15 family, free for kids under 11. Free admission to services. Mon–Sat 9:30am–3:45pm; Sun 2–5pm. Tube: Westminster.

❷ ★★★ Big Ben.
The iconic clock tower at the eastern end of the Palace of Westminster is mistakenly called Big Ben, though that appellation really refers to the largest bell in the clock's chime. The 14-ton bell,

The name Big Ben actually refers to the bell in the famous clock's chime.

installed in 1858, is believed to have been named for the commissioner of public works at the time—Sir Benjamin Charles—although some historians insist it was named for a famous boxer of the era, Benjamin Caunt. Brits can make the ascent up the tower's 334 spiral steps by special guided tour, but non-U.K. citizens must content themselves with a must-have snapshot. ⏲ 5 min. *Near St. Stephen's Entrance of Westminster Palace, Old Palace Yard. British citizens should contact their local MP to apply for permission to tour the clock tower.*

The Palace of Westminster, home to both Houses of Parliament.

❸ ★★ **Houses of Parliament.** The immense 3-hectare (8-acre) Palace of Westminster, a splendid example of Gothic Revival architecture, dates back to 1840 (the original palace was all but destroyed by fire in 1834). It's the home of the 659-member House of Commons (where elected officials do their legislating) and the 1,000-plus-member House of Lords (where descendants of royal mistresses and landed gentry do a lot of talking). You may observe debates for free from the **Stranger's Galleries** in both houses, but the long entry lines make this spot better for a quick photo op than a lengthy visit. The only exception: U.K. citizens can take worthwhile guided tours of the premises on select days throughout the year; non-U.K. citizens can take a guided tour only during Parliament's summer break. ⏲ 5 min. *Old Palace Yard.* ☎ *0207/219-3000 House of Commons; 0207/219-3107 House of Lords. www.parliament.uk. Free admission.*

Mon–Wed 2:30–10:30pm; Thurs 11:30am–7:30pm; Fri 9:30am–3pm. Closed Easter week. Guided tours (£7 adults, £5 kids 16 & under) offered to non-U.K. residents July–Oct only (check website or call for exact tour times). Tube: Westminster.

❹ ★ **The Jewel Tower.** This medieval structure was one of only two buildings to survive an 1834 fire that destroyed the original Palace of Westminster. The tower dates back to 1365 and was originally used to house Edward III's wardrobe and treasures. Today, it's home to a very informative exhibit, "Parliament Past & Present," which details the inner workings of the British government. Look carefully at the building's exterior as you enter and you'll spot the remains of a moat. ⏲ *25 min. Abingdon St.* ☎ *0207/222-2219. www. english-heritage.org.uk. Admission £2.20 adults, £1.10 kids 12 & under. Apr–Oct daily 10am–5pm; Nov–Mar daily 10am–4pm.*

The medieval Jewel Tower was once the treasure house of Edward III.

5 **Westminster Bridge.** From the center of this bridge you can enjoy a sweeping view of the Houses of Parliament and Big Ben—one of the most familiar and beloved cityscapes in the world. ⏱ *10 min. Tube: Westminster.*

6 ★ **Costa Coffee,** located behind the London Eye, is a quick-hit, outdoor cafe that provides heaters on the colder days. The sandwiches, panini, muffins, and drinks are all good, and the people-watching opportunities are endless. *Belvedere Rd.* ☎ *0207/401-7968. $*

7 ★★★ **kids** **British Airways London Eye.** The huge Ferris wheel that solemnly rotates at one revolution per half-hour is London's newest icon. It graces the skyscape from as far away as Hyde Park, and is much loved by even the most hardened London traditionalists. Although it was originally planned for only a 5-year stint, there's no way the London Tourist Board will let it go. You are encouraged to buy your timed ticket well in advance, which can end up in disappointment if you get a gray and rainy day. You may, however, be able to buy same-day tickets during the off season, which can eliminate the guesswork about the weather. Show up 30 minutes before your scheduled departure time (15 if you have a Fast Track ticket). Don't forget your camera. ⏱ *1 hr., from lining up through half-hour ride. Book*

The British London Eye offers some of the best views in London.

Fast Track tickets via the website or in person for double the price. Book through the website for a 5% discount. South Bank (at Westminster Bridge). ☎ *0870/500-0600. www. londoneye.com. Admission £13 adults, £10 seniors, £6.50 kids 5–15, free for kids under 5. May–June daily 9:30am–8pm; July–Aug daily 9:30am–10pm; Sept–Apr daily 9:30am–8pm. Closed bank holidays and 3 weeks in Jan. Tube: Westminster.*

8 ★★★ **kids** **Shakespeare's Globe Theatre.** Even if you don't have tickets to a Shakespeare play (p 133), the Globe is a fascinating place to visit. It was rebuilt in painstaking detail on a parking lot near the site of the original theater (and only those tools authentic to the period of the original were used in its construction). It was at the Globe in the early 1600s that Shakespeare's comedies and tragedies were performed in daylight (as they are now) to delight the nobility (who sat in the tiers) as well as the rabble (who stood before the stage). You can choose either option when purchasing tickets, weighing comfort versus

Shakespeare's Globe Theatre is a perfect replica of the Bard's original.

proximity to the stage. Changing exhibits focus on related topics such as the frost fairs of medieval London (back when the Thames would freeze into solid terrain, and people would party on the river for days); or the juicy history of nearby Southwark, once a haven for prostitutes, thieves, and actors. ⏲ 1 hr. 21 New Globe Walk. ☎ 0207/902-1500 (exhibition) or 0207/401-9919 (box office). www.shakespeares-globe.org. Admission to museum & exhibits: £8.50 adults, £7 seniors, £6 kids 5–15, £25 family (2 adults & 3 kids). Daily 10am–5pm (closed during afternoon theater matinees—call for schedules). Tube: London Bridge.

The 🍴 ★★ kids Globe Café is a fine choice for a restorative tea and sandwich, along with a Thames-side view of London. The menu features deliciously prepared English favorites, such as cottage pies, as well as more modern sandwiches and salads. 21 Globe Walk, SE1 (off Thames Path). ☎ 0207/902-1576. $

⓿ ★★★ kids Millennium Bridge. This gorgeous sliver of a footbridge connecting Bankside to The City and its attractions is an efficient way to cross the river and a wonderful spot from which to take photos of the surrounding landmarks. When it first opened in 2000, it swayed uncontrollably and had to be shut down, but it has since been stabilized. ⏲ 10 min. Tube: Southwark or Blackfriars.

⓫ ★★★ kids St. Paul's Cathedral. For centuries, the Dome of St. Paul's had no competition in the skyline of London; it was the highest and most impressive building in town. Though it has since been dwarfed by the skyscrapers in the financial district, none of them inspires the same awe as Sir

The ultramodern Millennium Bridge is one of the cities newest landmarks.

Christopher Wren's masterpiece, built after the Great Fire of 1666. The cathedral is the culmination of Wren's unique and much-acclaimed fusion of classical (the exterior Greek-style columns) and baroque (the ornate interior decorations) architecture. The Whispering Gallery is a miracle of engineering, in which you can hear the murmurs of another person from across a large gallery. The 530 stairs to the top are demanding, but you'll be rewarded with a magnificent view, not only of London, but of the marvel of the cathedral, which Wren—who is buried alongside many notable scientists and artists in the church's crypt—considered his ultimate achievement and most demanding effort. There are guided tours at 11am, 11:30am, 1:30pm, and 2pm. ⏲ ½ hr. Ludgate Hill, EC4 (at Paternoster Sq.). ☎ 0207/236-4128. www.stpauls.co.uk. Admission £7 adults, £6 seniors, £3 kids under 16. Mon–Sat 8:30 am–4:30 pm. Tube: St. Paul's.

St. Paul's Cathedral, Sir Christopher Wren's crowning achievement.

The Best **in Two Days**

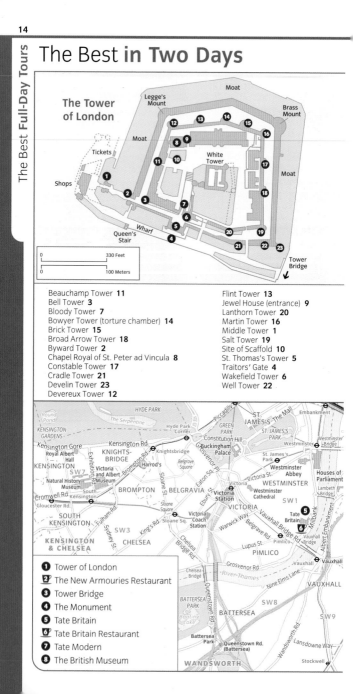

The Tower of London

Legge's Mount

Moat

Brass Mount

Moat

Tickets

White Tower

Shops

Moat

Wharf

Queen's Stair

| 0 | 330 Feet |
| 0 | 100 Meters |

Tower Bridge

Beauchamp Tower **11**
Bell Tower **3**
Bloody Tower **7**
Bowyer Tower (torture chamber) **14**
Brick Tower **15**
Broad Arrow Tower **18**
Byward Tower **2**
Chapel Royal of St. Peter ad Vincula **8**
Constable Tower **17**
Cradle Tower **21**
Develin Tower **23**
Devereux Tower **12**

Flint Tower **13**
Jewel House (entrance) **9**
Lanthorn Tower **20**
Martin Tower **16**
Middle Tower **1**
Salt Tower **19**
Site of Scaffold **10**
St. Thomas's Tower **5**
Traitors' Gate **4**
Wakefield Tower **6**
Well Tower **22**

HYDE PARK
Round Pond
The Serpentine
KENSINGTON GARDENS
Hyde Park Corner
Piccadilly
ST. JAMES'S
The Mall
Embankment
GREEN PARK
ST. JAMES'S PARK
Constitution Hill
Kensington Gore
Royal Albert Hall
Kensington Rd.
Kensington Rd.
Knightsbridge
Buckingham Palace
Westminster
Westminster Bridge
KNIGHTS-BRIDGE
St. James's Park
Belgrave Square
Grosvenor Pl.
St. James's St.
KENSINGTON
SW7
Exhibition Rd.
Brompton Rd.
Harrod's
Westminster Abbey
Natural History Museum
Victoria and Albert Museum
BROMPTON
BELGRAVIA
WESTMINSTER
Cromwell Rd.
South Kensington
Sloane St.
Eaton Sq.
Ebury St.
Victoria Station
Victoria
Westminster Cathedral
Lambeth Bridge
Gloucester Rd.
SOUTH KENSINGTON
Sloane Square
Sloane Sq.
Victoria Coach Station
VICTORIA
SW1
Tate Britain
Sydney St.
Fulham Rd.
King's Rd.
Warwick Way
Belgrave Rd.
Vauxhall Bridge Rd.
Millbank
KENSINGTON & CHELSEA
SW3
CHELSEA
Chelsea Bridge Rd.
Lupus St.
Pimlico
Vauxhall Bridge
Albert Embankment
Chelsea Bridge
PIMLICO
Grosvenor Rd.
Vauxhall
Vauxhall
BATTERSEA PARK
River Thames
Nine Elms Lane
VAUXHALL
Boating Lake
BATTERSEA
SW8
SW9
Battersea Park
Queenstown Rd. (Battersea)
Queenstown Rd.
Wandsworth Rd.
Lansdowne Way
WANDSWORTH
Stockwell

1 Tower of London
2 The New Armouries Restaurant
3 Tower Bridge
4 The Monument
5 Tate Britain
6 Tate Britain Restaurant
7 Tate Modern
8 The British Museum

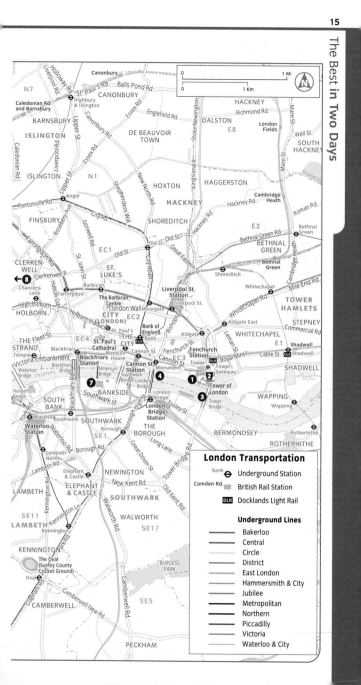

London Transportation

Bank   **⊖**   Underground Station

Camden Rd.   🚉   British Rail Station

DLR   Docklands Light Rail

Underground Lines

——— Bakerloo
——— Central
········· Circle
——— District
——— East London
——— Hammersmith & City
——— Jubilee
——— Metropolitan
——— Northern
——— Piccadilly
——— Victoria
——— Waterloo & City

On your second day in London, you will circle the globe and leap across centuries without ever leaving the city precincts. Even blasé Londoners are excited by the cauldron of history that is the Tower of London, the spoils of the Empire at the British Museum, the view from the top of the Monument, and the 21st-century art ensconced at the Tate Modern. And as a bonus, you get to traverse the Thames by boat. START: **Tower Hill Tube Station**

❶ ★★★ kids Tower of London.

Built by William the Conqueror in 1066, this fortress was added to by subsequent generations of kings and queens up to the Victorian Age, and is now an incomparable collection of buildings that reflect the range of England's architectural styles over the past millennium. The Tower has a bloody past marked by power struggles, executions, and cruelty: The young nephews of Richard III were murdered here in 1483; two of Henry VIII's six wives (Anne Boleyn and Catherine Howard) were beheaded on Tower Green, as was the 9-day queen, Lady Jane Grey; and Sir Walter Raleigh left his name on a walkway by his prison cell. Yeoman Guards (or "Beefeaters") give sprightly talks all day long, and talented actors offer living history lessons as they wander about in period costumes. The Crown Jewels are the most popular sight, just edging out the Torture Exhibit; the two together represent the awful accoutrements of power (and have the longest lines). The Tower, quite justifiably regarded as one of the most haunted—and haunting—places in London, will thrill students of history, and entertain kids as well.

The Tower of London is actually a fortress encompassing many buildings.

arrive before 9am to avoid the long lines; it's well worth the £3 handling charge. Tower Hill. ☎ *0870/756-6000. www.hrp.org.uk. Admission £14 adults, £11 seniors, £9 kids 5–15, free for kids under 5. Open daily 9am–6pm; till 5pm Nov–Feb. Tube: Tower Hill.*

Buy take-away sandwiches and drinks at ❷ ★★ **The New Armouries Restaurant** for an outdoor picnic, or settle in for a hot lunch of shepherd's pie, soup, Yorkshire pudding, or whatever you fancy. It's clean and pleasant though not hugely atmospheric. There are also snack shops scattered here and there around the Tower. *Inside the Tower of London.* ☎ *0870/756-6000.* $

🕐 *3 hr. Buy your tickets online &*

The Imperial State Crown, one of England's famous Crown Jewels.

3 ★★ **kids** **Tower Bridge.** This picture-perfect bascule bridge—a term derived from the French for "see-saw"—has spanned the Thames since 1894. There's no denying the physical beauty of the neo-Gothic bridge: Its skeleton of steel girders is clothed with ornate masonry using Cornish granite and Portland stone designed to harmonize elegantly with the neighboring Tower of London. Its lower span opens and closes thanks to hydraulics and behemoth machinery—details that even engineering-challenged visitors will find fascinating on the "Tower Bridge Experience" tour. Tour participants can also ascend to the bridge's top level for a bird's-eye view of the Tower of London and the Thames, 43m (140 ft.) below. (Acrophobics

Tower Bridge, not London Bridge, is the most recognizable bridge in the city.

need not apply.) ⏱ *1 hr. Tower Bridge.* ☎ *0207/403-3761. www. towerbridge.org.uk. £5.50 adults, £4.25 seniors, £3 kids 5–15. Ticket office is on northwest side of the bridge. Daily 9:30am–6pm. Tube: Tower Hill.*

Tower Ghosts

The Tower of London, said to be the most haunted spot in England, fairly overflows with supernatural manifestations of tormented souls.

The restless ghost of Queen Anne Boleyn (executed in 1536 on a trumped-up charge of treason after she'd failed to produce a male heir for Henry VIII) is the most frequently spotted spirit. The shades of the Little Princes (the two sons of Edward IV)—allegedly murdered by Richard III in 1483—have been spied in the Bloody Tower. Ghostly re-enactments of the Tower Green beheading of the Countess of Salisbury—who was hacked to death by her executioner on May 27, 1541—have been seen on its anniversary. The ghostly screams of Guy Fawkes, who gave up his co-conspirators in the Gunpowder Plot after suffering unspeakable torture, still echo around the grounds.

Other notable spirits you may encounter (the no-nonsense Tower guards have had run-ins with them all) include St. Thomas á Becket, Sir Walter Raleigh, Lady Jane Grey, and Henry VI.

One of the Tower of London's famous resident ravens.

④ ★ kids The Monument. Sir Christopher Wren and Robert Hooke designed this 62m-high (202-ft.) Doric stone column—topped with a copper flame—to commemorate the Great Fire of 1666. That tragic disaster started on September 2 inside the house of a baker on Pudding Lane (the height of the tower corresponds to the distance from its base to the fire's starting point). A stiff wind ignited the old timber and thatch houses of medieval London; when the conflagration was finally stopped, more than 13,000 houses and 87 churches had been reduced to smoldering ashes. Given the tower's 311 spiral steps, a climb to the top is not for the fainthearted, but if you make it, you'll be rewarded with a fabulous view of The City. ⏱ *30 min. Monument St.* ☎ *0207/626-2717.*

The Monument was built to commemorate the Great Fire of 1666.

www.towerbridge.org.uk. Admission £2 adults, £1 seniors & kids. Daily 9:30am–5:30pm. Tube: Monument.

Sailing the Tate Boat

The Tate boat ferry service between the two Tate museums on opposite banks of the Thames is one of London's better tourist creations. The same folks who built the London Eye designed the ferry's dramatic Millbank Pier, and the colorful catamaran is itself a work of art decorated by bad boy artist Damian Hirst. The 18-minute ride runs from the Tate Britain to the Tate Modern, and also makes a stop at the British Airways London Eye (p 12, bullet ⑦). When you're visiting both Tate museums in a single day, the ferry is a convenient, scenic, and comfortable way to get from one to the other.

Alas, it's not free. One-way ferry tickets cost £3.40 adults, £1.70 kids under 16, free for kids under 5. If you have a London Travelcard (p 157), you get a 33% discount. Tickets can be bought online or at the Tate Britain or Tate Modern. The boat runs daily every 40 minutes (more often in high season) between 10am and 6pm. For precise boat times, call ☎ 0207/887-3959 or check www.tate.org.uk/tatetotate.

The Tate Britain lit up at night.

5 ★★ kids **Tate Britain.** The Tate Britain, set on the former Thames-side site of the Millbank Penitentiary, opened in 1894 thanks to generous donations of money and art from sugar mogul Sir Henry Tate. One of England's most prestigious art museums, the Tate features a collection consisting chiefly of British art from the 16th century to the dawn of the 20th century. The museum has an unparalleled collection of works by renowned landscape artist J. M. W. Turner, who bequeathed most of his paintings to the museum. Other notable British artists whose works adorn the walls include satirist William Hogarth, illustrator William Blake, portraitist Thomas Gainsborough, and traditionalist Joshua Reynolds. ⏲ *2 hr. Millbank.* ☎ *0207/887-8008. www. tate.org.uk. Free admission, except for temporary exhibits. Daily 10am–6pm. Tube: Pimlico.*

The **6** ★★ **Tate Britain Restaurant** is one of the best museum eateries in London, and serves tasty modern British cuisine, accompanied by an extensive wine list, in a cheery, mural-filled dining room. It's a great place to stop for afternoon tea. *In the Tate Britain.* ☎ *0207/ 887-8825. $$*

Matisse's The Snail, *in the Tate Modern.*

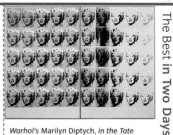

Warhol's Marilyn Diptych, *in the Tate Modern.*

7 ★★★ kids **Tate Modern.** Britain's premier modern art museum, an offshoot of the Tate Britain, is housed in a gargantuan shell that was once a power station. For me, part of the fun of a visit here is reminiscing about the building's past—check out the immensity of the Turbine Hall and wonder at the amount of electricity once needed to power the lights in London. The museum's curators have admirably risen to the challenge of filling its enormous space with exhibits, gigantic sculptures, and art installations. Collections here are displayed thematically instead of by period. Highlights include a time-lapse fruit bowl video by Sam Taylor-Wood, and works by Dalí, Picasso, Mondrian, and Hockney. I also find the permanent exhibit of everyday items recovered from the Thames during the building's transformation into a museum strangely riveting. ⏲ *1½ hr. Take a free guided theme tour or an audioguide highlights tour (£2) to make the best use of your time. Bankside.* ☎ *0207/887-8000. www.tate.org.uk. Free admission except for temporary exhibits. Daily 10am–6pm. Tube: Blackfriars.*

8 ★★★ kids **The British Museum.** You could spend days exploring this renowned museum, but if you're touring on a Thursday or Friday, when it's open late, end your day in its Egyptian and Asian galleries. ⏲ *1 hr. See p 32, bullet* **10***; & p 33, bullet* **11***.*

The Best **in Three Days**

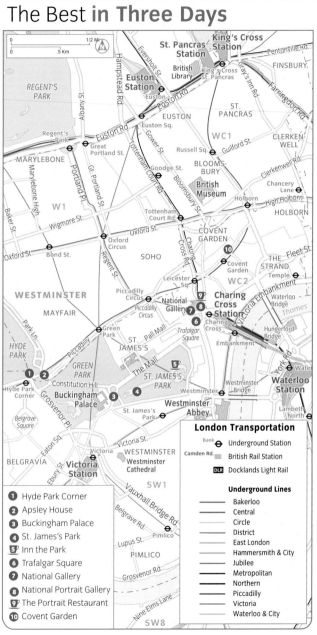

1 Hyde Park Corner
2 Apsley House
3 Buckingham Palace
4 St. James's Park
5 Inn the Park
6 Trafalgar Square
7 National Gallery
8 National Portrait Gallery
9 The Portrait Restaurant
10 Covent Garden

London Transportation

Bank ⊖ Underground Station
Camden Rd. ▇ British Rail Station
DLR Docklands Light Rail

Underground Lines

— Bakerloo
— Central
— Circle
— District
— East London
— Hammersmith & City
— Jubilee
— Metropolitan
— Northern
— Piccadilly
— Victoria
— Waterloo & City

This tour reveals London's great charms. I follow this route when I'm feeling out of sorts, and by the time I hit St. James's Park, I've fallen in love with London all over again. From the glory of Hyde Park Corner's monuments, to the incomparable art in the National Gallery, to the street crazies of Covent Garden, this is the London that even crabby cabbies quietly relish as they go about their business. START: **Hyde Park Corner Tube Station**

1 ★ Hyde Park Corner. The busiest traffic circle in London is one of the city's most central locations, with Piccadilly, Knightsbridge, Park Lane, Constitution Hill, and Grosvenor Place radiating from its axis. It's the perfect place to get great morning photos of the majestic statue of *Winged Victory*, which replaced the statue of the Duke of Wellington in 1912 as a topper to the Wellington Arch. The arch itself was built in the 1820s to celebrate the British victory over the French. The underground walkways beneath the circle will save you from the treacherous crosswalks above and feature an interesting pictorial history of the Duke of Wellington, who orchestrated the crushing of Napoleon at Waterloo and remains one of Britain's most celebrated military heroes. ⏱ *10 min. Tube: Hyde Park Corner.*

2 ★★ Apsley House. Designed by famed architect Robert Adam, this neoclassical mansion was purchased by Arthur Wellesley, first Duke of Wellington (1769–1852), following his victories in the Napoleonic Wars. Its location, just past the old Knightsbridge toll-gate, gave it the city's most grandiose address at the time: Number One London. The residence houses a renowned collection of decorative arts (many of the

The dining room at Apsley House and its priceless Portuguese silver centerpiece.

pieces bestowed upon the duke by grateful European monarchs), historic weaponry, numerous Old Masters, a towering nude statue of his enemy Napoleon (with a strategic fig leaf), and some charming views of Hyde Park. It's a small, quick-hit museum that provides you with a taste of old Georgian splendor (don't miss the staggeringly over-the-top silver table setting, with an 8m-long [27-ft.] centerpiece). ⏱ *30 min. 149 Piccadilly.* ☎ *0207/499-5676. www.english-heritage.org. uk. Admission £4.50 adults, £3 seniors, £2.30 kids 5–15. Tues–Sun 10am–5pm. Tube: Hyde Park Corner.*

Wellington Arch, topped by the Winged Victory, sits atop Hyde Park Corner.

The Changing of the Guard at Buckingham Palace.

❸ ★ Buckingham Palace. Buck House, the queen's famous abode in London (if the flag is flying, it means she's there), is the setting for the pageantry of the **Changing of the Guard,** a London tradition that attracts more people than it warrants—it's a nightmarish mass of crowds in the summer. A better place to see all the queen's horses and all the queen's men in action is the Horse Guards Parade (p 69, bullet ❸). But if you're determined to see the guards change here, arrive a half-hour early for a seat on the statue of Victoria in front of the palace; it offers a reasonably good view. The ritual takes place every other day in winter and every day in summer at 11am in the forecourt of the palace. ⏱ *30 min. See p 45, bullet ❶.*

❹ ★★ kids St. James's Park. Arguably London's prettiest park, St. James's has an interesting history. The former swamp was tidied up in the 18th century, after it became a notorious scene where prostitutes conducted business, laundresses brought their loads to dry on bushes, and drunken rakes took unsteady aim at dueling opponents. Now, however, it's very respectable, with a duck and pelican pond, weeping willows, and numerous paths lined with flower beds. The benches at the eastern end of the park offer a peaceful view of London's landmarks. ⏱ *30 min.*

At the northeast end of St. James's Park is **❺ ★★ kids Inn the Park,** a combination cafe and restaurant. Skip the expensive restaurant, where the food is overpriced; the same chefs supply the less-expensive cafeteria-style eatery, which features glorious views of the London Eye and Whitehall. *In St James's Park (by Pall Mall).* ☎ *0207/451-9999. $*

❻ Trafalgar Square. While you were once able to identify this famous square by its preponderance of pigeons, the practice of feeding them was outlawed, and the pigeons now crowd the grass in front of the National Gallery. The square is named after Britain's most revered naval hero, Horatio Viscount Nelson, who fell at the Battle of Trafalgar (the most pivotal naval battle of the Napoleonic Wars) in 1805, and whose stone statue stands on top of a 44m (144-ft.) pillar of granite guarded by kingly lions at the base. Street lamps at the Pall Mall end of the square are decorated with small replicas of the ships he commanded. The square is the scene of many rallies, demonstrations, and celebrations, and it's perfect for people-watching.

❼ ★★★ kids National Gallery. This famous museum dominating Trafalgar Square sits roughly where the stables of King Henry VIII used to be. Founded in 1832 with a collection of 38 paintings bought by the English government, National is now home to some 2,000 works

The statue of Horatio Viscount Nelson overlooking Trafalgar Square.

representing the world's major artistic periods from 1250 to 1900. It's London's best museum for anyone interested in the arts.

National Gallery Highlights

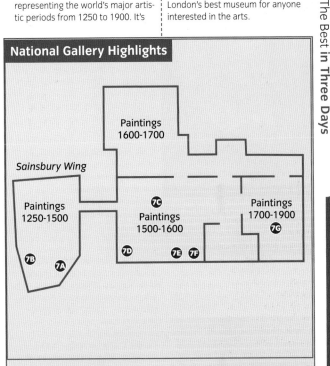

Paintings 1600-1700

Sainsbury Wing

Paintings 1250-1500

7C Paintings 1500-1600

Paintings 1700-1900 **7G**

7B **7A**

7D **7E** **7F**

Start in the **7A** ★★★ **Sainsbury Wing's Room 56,** where you'll find familiar early European works, including Van Eyck's haunting portrait, *Arnolfini and His Wife.* Note the words inscribed over the mirror: "Jan Van Eyck was here/1434." For a contrast in mood, go to **7B Room 66** for Botticelli's *Venus & Mars,* a voluptuous allegory most likely painted as a backboard to decorate a bench or chest. The **7C West Wing's Room 10** holds Titian's *Bacchus & Ariadne* in colors still vibrant after 500 years. In **7D Room 8** is an ethereal Raphael painting of *St. Catherine.* Holbein's

Ambassadors is in **7E Room 4;** the skull in the foreground was painted with a geometrical process called *anamorphosis,* distorting the image unless you look at it from an angle. Pay your respects to Michelangelo and da Vinci in **7F Room 2,** and then leave the Renaissance for the **7G East Wing** to see the works of Impressionists van Gogh, Monet, and Seurat, among others.

🕐 *2 hr. Trafalgar Sq. (at St. Martin's Lane).* ☎ *0207/747-2285. www. nationalgallery.org.uk. Free admission, except for temporary exhibits. Thurs–Tues 10am–6pm; Wed 10am–9pm. Tube: Leicester Sq.*

A portrait of William Shakespeare at the National Portrait Gallery.

⑧ ★★ kids National Portrait Gallery. Adjacent to the National Gallery, the NPG is the best place to put a face to the names of those who have shaped England politically, socially, and culturally. The gallery displays 2,400 portraits at any given time, ranging from King Henry VII to designer Vivienne Westwood. Exhibitions tend toward the fabulous, with shows featuring such renowned photographers as Sir Cecil Beaton, Julia Cameron, and Mario Testino. Start at the top and work your way down. ⏱ *1 hr. 2 St. Martin's Lane, W1.* ☎ *0207/306-0055. www.npg. org.uk. Free admission, except for temporary exhibits. Sat–Wed 10am–6pm; Thurs–Fri 10am–9pm. Tube: Leicester Sq.*

⑨ ★★★ The Portrait Restaurant, on the top floor of the NPG, commands the most spectacular views over Trafalgar Square. The lounge area, serving salads, light meals, and afternoon tea, is your best bet for a quick bite. *National Portrait Gallery, 2 St. Martin's Lane, W1.* ☎ *0207/312-2490. $$*

⑩ ★★★ kids Covent Garden. When you've had enough of culture, and you fancy a bit of shopping, this famous marketplace—first laid out in the 17th century—is a good spot to end your day's explorations. The area is roughly bordered by the Strand, Charing Cross, Drury Lane, and High Holborn. At its heart is the Inigo Jones–designed arcade now filled with upscale shops and uninspired cafes. **Jubilee Market,** with inexpensive what-nots and cheap clothing, is set on the southern side of the arcade; at the western end you'll find stalls that, depending on the day, offer antiques, handmade crafts, or flea-market goods. You may even be lucky enough to come upon an operatic performance given by professionals from the neoclassical **Royal Opera House** that faces the arcade. This area offers busking at its best; be it a tattooed man juggling knives, or a chamber music quartet, you'll always find real talent in Covent Garden's street entertainment. ⏱ *1–2 hr. Tube: Covent Garden.* ●

Colorful Covent Garden is a good spot for shopping and street entertainment.

and let thy feet
millenniums hence
be set in midst of knowledge

Victoria and Albert Museum

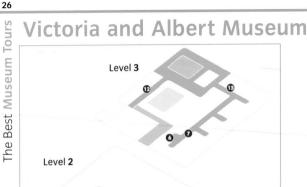

Level 3

Level 2

Level 1

Level 0

Exhibition Road Entrance

Cromwell Road Entrance

Tunnel Entrance

	Asia
	Europe
	Materials and Techniques
	Modern
	Exhibitions
	Garden

❶ Chihuly Glass Chandelier	❾ Cast Courts
❷ The British Galleries	☕ Gamble Room Café
❸ Beasts of Dacre	⓫ The Ceramic Staircase
❹ Raphael's Cartoons	⓬ Silver Gallery
❺ Fashion Gallery	⓭ Gilbert Bayes Sculpture Gallery
❻ Musical Instruments	⓮ Photography Gallery
❼ Ironwork Gallery	⓯ Renaissance Galleries
❽ Sculpture Gallery	☕ Museum Café

This museum's 13km (8 miles) of corridors are resplendent with the world's greatest collection of decorative arts. Opened in 1852 by Prince Albert, this treasure trove, known as the V&A, is now home to millions of priceless artworks from around the world, including paintings, furniture, glass, ceramics, silver, and fashion. START: **Tube to South Kensington**

1 ★★★ Chihuly Glass Chandelier. Renowned glass artist Dale Chihuly created this serpentine green and blue masterpiece specifically for the V&A in 2001, when an exhibition of his work was staged in the museum's Perelli Courtyard. It's 8m (27 ft.) long, and made up of thousands of exquisite hand-blown glass baubles. Despite its airy effect, it weighs 3,800 pounds. *Foyer.* ⏱ *3 min.*

The Great Bed of Ware is one of the V&A's top treasures.

2 ★★★ kids The British Galleries. This stellar example of 21st-century curatorship features some of England's greatest cultural treasures. The big draw is the **Great Bed of Ware** (Room 57), a masterpiece of woodcarving that earned mention by Shakespeare in *Twelfth Night.* Built in 1596 as a gimmick for an inn, the bed is now covered in I WAS HERE graffiti and wax seals left by centuries of visitors. Another highlight is the *Portrait of Margaret Laton* (Room 56); the painting is rather ordinary, but the jacket displayed alongside it is the very one worn in the portrait, which makes a stop here worthwhile. The interactive area will quell any kids' rebellions; my favorite display allows you to design your own heraldic crest on a computer. ⏱ *1 hr.*

3 ★★ Beasts of Dacre. These four carved heraldic animals (gryphon, bull, dolphin, and ram) were carved for the Dacres, one of northern England's most important families, in 1520. The wooden figures survived a fire in 1844, only to be restored in a rather gaudy, carousel-animal, Victorian style. Their weird whimsy has a wondrous dignity. *Stairway C.* ⏱ *5 min.*

4 ★★★ Raphael's Cartoons. Dating back to 1521, these immense and expertly rendered drawings (*cartoon* is derived from the Italian word for a large piece of paper, *cartone*)

A heraldic bull, one of the Beasts of Dacre.

were used by the artist Raphael to plot a set of tapestries originally intended to hang in the Vatican's Sistine Chapel. *Room 48a.* 🕐 *15 min.*

5 ★★ **Fashion Gallery.** From a ludicrous 18th-century, 1.2m-wide (4-ft.) skirt to vertiginous platform shoes by Vivienne Westwood, this gallery is proof positive that every age has its share of fashion victims. *Room 40.* 🕐 *25 min.*

6 ★ **Musical Instruments.** This gallery displays a first-class collection of ivory and ebony inlaid guitars and lutes, as well as spinets, pianos, and virginals (including Elizabeth I's 1570 model—the Virgin Queen was reportedly quite the accomplished musician) that have been decorated to within an inch of their lives. *Room 40a.* 🕐 *20 min.*

7 ★★ **Ironwork Gallery.** Just past curlicued gates and a nostalgic display of cookie tins, you'll find this gallery's highlight—the stupendous **Hereford Screen,** a masterpiece of Victorian ironwork designed by the same man who devised the Albert Memorial (p 46, bullet **5**). Check out the bird's-eye view of the foyer's chandelier. *Room 114.* 🕐 *20 min.*

8 ★★ **Sculpture Gallery.** Sarcophagi, marble founts, and alabaster busts of great beauty are just some of the treasures you'll find in this gallery. *Room 50a.* 🕐 *20 min.*

9 ★★★ **Cast Courts.** These two popular rooms used to be more colorfully titled "Fakes and Forgeries." Some of the counterfeit items are exceptional, executed with just as much skill as the originals. Among the imitations, you'll find a plaster cast of the statue of David (whose nudity so shocked Queen Victoria, she had a fig leaf made for it—it's now displayed behind the statue), a copy of Ghiberti's famous bronze doors for Florence's Baptistery, and

An 18th-century gown from the Fashion Gallery.

an entire church facade. *Rooms 46a & 46b.* 🕐 *20 min.*

For a quick snack in gorgeous surroundings, stop for sandwiches, salads, or desserts at the ornate **10** **Gamble Room Café,** the world's first museum cafe (opened in 1868). The eatery's stained-glass windows tell the story of the seasons. *Off Rooms 13–15. $*

11 ★★ **The Ceramic Staircase.** The V&A's first director, Henry Cole, designed these stairs, intending to doll up all the museum's staircases in this ceramics-gone-mad style. For better or worse, when the costs for the staircase spiraled out of control in 1870, the project was quietly dropped. *Staircase I.* 🕐 *10 min.*

12 ★★ **Silver Gallery.** Find treasure beyond measure in a jaw-dropping array of over 10,000 silver objects, ranging from baby rattles to candelabras. Highlights include the 19th-century (and gem-encrusted)

The ornate Burgess Cup is just one of the V&A's silver treasures.

Burgess Cup; and a rare, engraved 17th-century silver flask that belonged to the first Duke of Albans, the illegitimate son of Charles II and his mistress, actress Nell Gwynn. Interactive educational displays will teach you more about the precious metal than you may want to know. *Rooms 65–70a.* 🕐 *25 min.*

⓭ ★★ **Gilbert Bayes Sculpture Gallery.** This collection of small European sculpture in every imaginable medium is in an enviable position: It's off the elegant but dimly lit Leighton Hall (check out the floor tiles) and gives you a tree-top view of the Cast Courts, allowing you to inspect the dramatic details on the top of the stone church facade, below. *Room 111.* 🕐 *20 min.*

⓮ ★★★ **Photography Gallery.** The V&A's vast and outstanding collection of images (some 300,000) was started in 1852. Works from as far back as 1839 are shown on a rotating basis. You might see prints by noted British shutterbugs Julia Cameron and Bill Brandt, or early daguerreotypes. *Room 38a.* 🕐 *15 min.*

⓯ ★★★ **Renaissance Galleries.** A mélange of mediums from the creatively fertile Renaissance era (1200–1650) is on display here, including tapestries, stained glass, statuary, glass, and metalwork. Notable items include a 15th-century Murano glass goblet and a 15th-century stained glass panel of Holy Roman Emperor Maximilian I that originally hung in Bruges' Chapel of the Holy Blood. *Rooms 21–25.* 🕐 *30 min.*

Stop at the ⓰ **Museum Café** for good-quality food—traditional English fare, plus sandwiches and salads—at cafeteria prices. The teatime desserts at this self-service eatery are excellent, as are the homemade scones. *Level 0.* $

The V&A: Practical Matters

The Victoria and Albert Museum (☎ 0207/942-2000; www.vam.ac.uk) is located at Cromwell Road, SW7, off Exhibition Road. Take the Tube to South Kensington and follow the signs to the museum.

Admission is free, except to special exhibits. The museum is open daily from 10am to 5:45pm. On Wednesday, the V&A stays open until 10pm for the Late View, when live music, guided tours, and lectures are offered (it's best for adults). On weekends, there are special activities for kids of all ages.

The British Museum

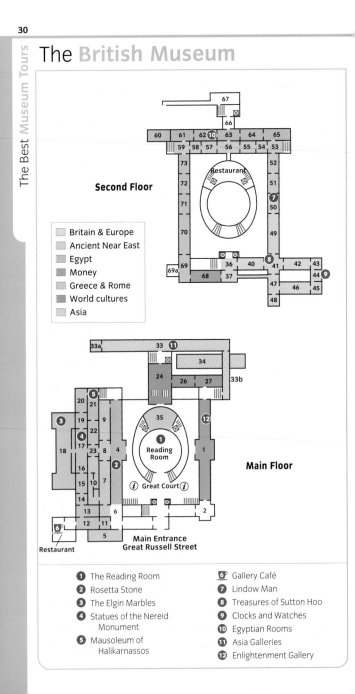

Second Floor

Britain & Europe
Ancient Near East
Egypt
Money
Greece & Rome
World cultures
Asia

Restaurant

Main Floor

Main Entrance
Great Russell Street

Restaurant

❶ The Reading Room
❷ Rosetta Stone
❸ The Elgin Marbles
❹ Statues of the Nereid Monument
❺ Mausoleum of Halikarnassos

❻ Gallery Café
❼ Lindow Man
❽ Treasures of Sutton Hoo
❾ Clocks and Watches
❿ Egyptian Rooms
⓫ Asia Galleries
⓬ Enlightenment Gallery

The British Museum, started with a donation by collector Sir Hans Sloane in 1753, opened at a time when the expansion of the British Empire into just about every corner of the earth ensured that its collection would be as eclectic as it was priceless. Note the frieze above the entrance—it signifies the museum's intention to encompass all the branches of science and art. START: **Holborn Tube Station**

1 ★★ The Reading Room. This hallowed place of literary history has been restored to its 1857 grandeur. If the circular stacks of books and the crowning gilt-and-azure dome don't get you, turn around and look on either side of the entrance doors. You'll find a list of authors (Dickens, Marx, Tennyson, Kipling, and Darwin, among others) who sat in this very room to write, think, and research some of literature's finest works. There's a children's section, but quiet must be observed. A free multimedia database here allows you to search the museum's vast collections. ⏱ *15 min.*

2 ★★★ Rosetta Stone. One of the museum's most highly prized artifacts is an ancient text engraved on a tablet in three scripts (hieroglyphic, demotic, and Greek) and two languages (Greek and Egyptian) that enumerates the virtues of 13-year-old pharaoh Ptolemy V, who lived in 196 B.C. The tablet was found in 1799 by Napoleon's troops and handed over to the British Army as part of the Alexandria Treaty of 1802. The text was deciphered in 1822, a breakthrough that allowed archaeologists and historians to decode ancient Middle Eastern hieroglyphics, and proved that these

A frieze from the Parthenon, one of the famous Elgin Marbles.

symbols represented a spoken language. *Room 4.* ⏱ *5 min.*

3 ★★★ The Elgin Marbles. The Greek government has been fighting for 2 centuries to get these detailed classical sculptures and artifacts—taken from the Parthenon by Lord Elgin in 1805—returned to Athens. The B.M. argues that it has provided a safe home for these carvings (including 75m/247 ft. of the original temple frieze), which would otherwise have been chipped away by vandals or degraded by remaining in the open air. The marbles may yet be returned to the Parthenon (a disastrous precedent for the museum, filled as it is with the booty of the world), but don't expect them to depart the B.M. anytime soon. *Room 18.* ⏱ *20 min.*

The Rosetta Stone, one of the most significant artifacts in the world.

④ ★ Statues of the Nereid Monument.

This 4th-century B.C. Lykian tomb from southwest Turkey arrived at the museum with the Elgin Marbles in 1816, and its lifelike statuary is almost surreal. Even without their heads, the daughters of the sea god Nereus (aka Nereids) look as graceful as the ocean waves they are meant to personify. *Room 17.* ⏱ *5 min.*

⑤ ★★ Mausoleum of Halikarnassos.

These are the remains of one of the Seven Wonders of the Ancient World—the breathtaking Ionian Greek tomb built for King Maussollos, from whose name the word "mausoleum" is derived. The tomb remained undisturbed from 351 B.C. to medieval times, when an earthquake damaged it. In 1494, Crusaders used its stones to fortify a castle refuge; in 1846, sections of the tomb's frieze were found at the castle and given to the B.M. Subsequent excavations turned up the remarkably lifelike horse sculpture and the series of lounging figures. *Room 21.* ⏱ *15 min.*

The excellent ⑥ ★★ **kids Gallery Café** is a relaxed, cafeteria-style eatery decorated with the 1801 casts of the Elgin Marbles. The hot meals, sandwiches, and desserts are all reasonably priced. *Off Room 12.* ☎ *0207/323-8990.* $

⑦ Lindow Man.

Don't miss the affecting cadaver of the "Bog Man" (aka "Pete Marsh"), preserved in a peat bog in Lindow Moss, Cheshire, for nearly 2,000 years (he was found in 1984). The poor man was struck on the head, garroted, knifed, and

An early Anglo-Saxon helmet that's one of the Treasures of Sutton Hoo.

then put head first into the bog! The excessiveness of his pre-mortem wounds suggests he died in a Druidic sacrificial ritual. *End of Room 50, on your right.* ⏱ *5 min.*

⑧ ★★★ Treasures of Sutton Hoo.

Sutton Hoo was a burial ground of the early Anglo-Saxons (including one royal, who literally went down with his 30m/98-ft. oak ship). When this tomb was excavated in 1939, previous beliefs about the inferior arts and crafts of England's Dark Age (ca. A.D. 625) were confounded, as well-designed musical instruments, glassware, armor, and even Byzantine articles (don't miss the exquisitely detailed Wilton Cross) were uncovered. *Room 41.* ⏱ *15 min.*

⑨ ★★ Clocks and Watches.

The museum's outstanding collection of timepieces features the mind-blowing Galleon (or "Nef") Clock, which used to roll along a table announcing dinnertime to guests. Built (in 1865 in Germany) to resemble a medieval galleon, the gilt-copper marvel played music, beat drums, and even fired tiny cannons for emphasis. *Room 44.* ⏱ *20 min.*

⑩ ★★★ Egyptian Rooms.

It's said that the ghost of one of the 3,000-year-old mummies on display roams these rooms. Room 62 has a **mummified cat,** while Room 63 is filled with brightly painted coffins and the **remains of Cleopatra**—who, by the miracle of modern imaging techniques, was determined to have been quite an unattractive woman. Room 64 has the shocking 5,000-year-old carcass of a man the museum calls "**Ginger,**" whose body dried out naturally in the desert (his preserved red hair earned him the nickname). ⏱ *30 min.*

⓫ ★★ Asia Galleries. Room 33 is an oasis of calm that lures you with the serenity of meditating Buddhas and the grace of the *Dancing Shiva*—a bronze sculpture depicting one of India's most famous images. The intricate frieze of the **Great Stupa** (Room 33a) carved in India in the 3rd century B.C. looks so much like the Elgin Marbles, you'll wonder about the artistic zeitgeist that seems to pass unaided through borders and cultures. There are statues of bodhisattvas, Buddhist archetypes, in every medium—from porcelain to metal. As you exit through Room 33b, be sure to look at the **Chinese jade carvings** (some are over 4,000 years old). ⏲ *20 min.*

The coffin of Cleopatra.

⓬ Enlightenment Gallery. "Discovering the World in the 18th Century" is the subtitle of this permanent exhibit, located in the restored King's Library. Designed for George III by Sir Robert Smirke, the room is regarded as the finest and largest neoclassical interior hall in London. You'll be reaching for your pince-nez and quill pen as you marvel at the polished mahogany bookshelves stuffed with rare books, and eagerly examine the display cases filled with some 5,000 items that demonstrate the far-reaching, eclectic passions of the 18th-century Enlightenment scholar—the exact kind of person who made the British Museum possible. ⏲ *30 min.*

Practical Matters

The British Museum (☎ 0207/636-1555; www.thebritishmuseum. ac.uk) is located on Great Russell Street. Take the Tube to the Tottenham Court Road, Russell Square, or Holborn station.

Admission is free, except for temporary special exhibits. The museum is open daily from 10am to 5:30pm; on Thursday and Friday, select galleries remain open until 8:30pm. A variety of specialty tours of the museum are offered, ranging from self-guided audio tours for families to free, 50-minute introductory tours; check the website for details or inquire at the Information Desk in the museum's Great Court. The website's "Compass" database offers access to data on thousands of the museum's objects.

Bronze figure of Nataraja (Dancing Shiva) in the Asian Galleries.

London's Best Small Museums

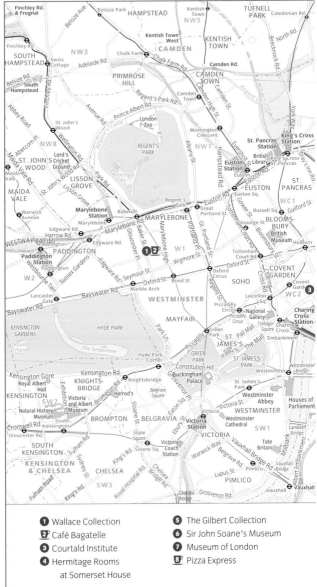

1 Wallace Collection
2 Café Bagatelle
3 Courtald Institute
4 Hermitage Rooms
   at Somerset House

5 The Gilbert Collection
6 Sir John Soane's Museum
7 Museum of London
8 Pizza Express

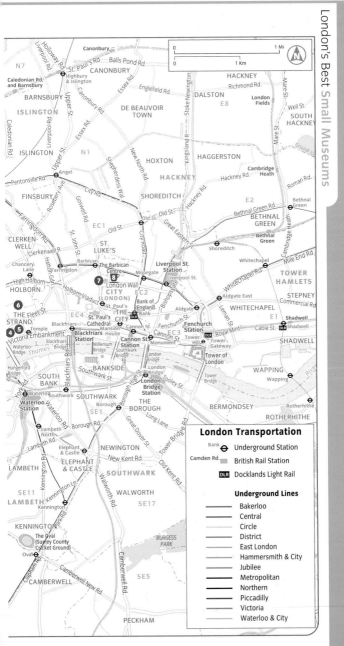

London Transportation

Bank ⊖	Underground Station
Camden Rd. ▪	British Rail Station
DLR	Docklands Light Rail

Underground Lines

———	Bakerloo
———	Central
———	Circle
———	District
———	East London
———	Hammersmith & City
———	Jubilee
———	Metropolitan
———	Northern
———	Piccadilly
———	Victoria
———	Waterloo & City

If, like me, you suffer from sore feet when visiting huge museums or you dislike milling crowds, you'll be delighted by the charms of London's many smaller museums. These are often housed in beautiful old mansions whose appealing architectural details can be as fascinating as the items on view. Most of these lesser-known gems aren't as mobbed by visitors, so you can take your time when inspecting the unique collections, which may reflect the taste of their original owners (Sir John Soane's Museum) or reveal the artistic leanings of an entire age (the Wallace Collection). START: **Bond St. Tube Station**

❶ ★★★ Wallace Collection.

This collection offers an astonishing glimpse into the buying power of the English gentry after the French Revolution, when important art works were made homeless by the guillotine. In the late 19th century, this entire mansion and its contents were left to the nation by Lady Wallace on the condition that they be kept intact, without additions or subtractions. The paintings are breathtaking, with works by Titian, Gainsborough, Rembrandt, Hals (including his famous *Laughing Cavalier*), and others. But the most fascinating aspect of the collection is the rare opportunity to view exceptional art in a house whose architectural details, fine furniture,

One of the Wallace Collection's ornately furnished rooms.

and Sèvres tableware give visitors a glimpse into a vanished aristocratic world. A recent renovation has upgraded the facilities, and their pleasant restaurant is a great place to refresh yourself. ⏱ *1 hr. Arrive at opening. Hertford House, Manchester Sq.* ☎ *0207/935-0687. www.the-wallace-collection.org.uk. Free admission. Open Mon–Sat 10am–5pm; Sun noon–5pm. Tube: Bond St.*

Pause at the Wallace Collection's airy ❷ ★★ **Café Bagatelle** which serves up tasty light meals inside a pleasant glass-covered and sculpture-filled atrium. It's a great place to rest your legs while indulging in a cup of tea. ☎ *0207/935-0687. $$*

❸ ★★ Courtald Institute.

Housed inside Somerset House, a Georgian romp of a chateau whose centerpiece is a public courtyard (with an ice rink in winter and a picturesque fountain in summer), the Courtald is a choice destination for art lovers. The institute is especially celebrated for its Impressionist collection (van Gogh's *Self-Portrait with Bandaged Ear* and Manet's second version of *Dejeuner Sur l'Herbe* are just two of its world-famous paintings), but it is also home to works by such notables as Botticelli, Rubens, and Brueghel. ⏱ *30 min.* ☎ *0207/ 848-2526. www.somerset-house. org.uk. Museum admission free Mon*

paintings once owned by the czars of Russia. Be sure to look at the Thames-side terrace's view of St. Paul's when you exit. 🕐 *30 min.* ☎ *0207/845-4630. www.somerset-house.org.uk. Admission £5 adults, £4 seniors, free to kids under 18. Joint discount tickets available (see bullet ❸). Daily 10am–6pm. Tube: Charing Cross.*

❺ ★★★ **kids** **The Gilbert Collection.** The last—and in many ways, most eclectic—of Somerset House's museums serves up a wild mix of gold, silver, jewels, mosaics, decorative furniture, and tchotchkes—all displayed in their most Arabian Nights abundance and glitter. The decorative arts collection here rivals that of the V&A in quality if not in quantity. The museum is also home to one of the most comprehensive collections of Italian mosaics in the world. Must-sees include a pair of very ornate Russian "royal gates" commissioned by Russia's Catherine the Great; a magnificent marble-and-gilt clock presented to Napoleon by Pope Pius VII in honor of his coronation as emperor; and a set of gem-encrusted gold snuffboxes made for Frederick the Great. 🕐 *1 hr. Somerset House, The Strand.* ☎ *0207/420-9400. www.gilbert-collection.org.uk. Admission £5 adults, £4 seniors, free to kids under 18. Joint discount tickets available (see bullet ❸). Daily 10am–6pm. Tube: Charing Cross.*

Van Gogh's Self-Portrait with Bandaged Ear, *in the Courtauld Institute.*

10am–2pm. Admission other days £5 adults, £4 seniors, free to kids under 18. Joint discount tickets for admission to all 3 Somerset House museums £12 adults, £11 seniors, free to kids under 18. Daily 10am–6pm. Tube: Charing Cross.

❹ ★★★ **Hermitage Rooms at Somerset House.** The second of Somerset's trio of museums features treasures from St. Petersburg's famous State Hermitage Museum in a setting meant to resemble that city's famous Winter Palace. The exhibitions change often (rare porcelain was on display when I was last there), but you may find yourself admiring Fabergé eggs, jewelry, furniture, and

One of the Gilbert Collection's jeweled snuffboxes.

The former home of Sir John Soane now displays the noted architect's collection of antiques and paintings.

⑥ ★★ Sir John Soane's Museum.

The distinguished British architect Sir John Soane (1753–1837) was also an avid collector. His former home in Lincoln Fields is a testament to his skill as an architect (the use of interior space enabled an immense number of antiquities and paintings to be stuffed into the house) and to the breadth of his hobby. The bulk of the collection was amassed between the late 18th and early 19th centuries, when antiquities could be removed from their country of origin and displayed casually in one's home. Ancient tablets, sculptures, paintings (including William Hogarth's celebrated *Rake's Progress*), architectural models, and even an Egyptian sarcophagus are strewn around in no particular order, and the haphazardness of the display is part of the museum's charm. ⏱ 1 hr. 13 Lincoln Inn Fields. ☎ 0207/405-2107.

www.soane.org. Free admission. Tues–Sat 10am–5pm. Tube: Holborn.

⑦ ★★★ kids Museum of London.

If it has to do with London's history, you'll find it at this incredibly comprehensive museum. Reconstructions of 19th-century shops and Anderson bomb shelters from World War II are just two of the time-travel displays at this wonderful location. The exhibits start at the prehistoric level and proceed to the 21st century, with stops at all the great and terrible moments of London's long life. Do not miss the ornate Lord Mayor's Coach, a 3-ton gilt affair in which Cinderella would have felt right at home. ⏱ 1½ hr. London Wall. ☎ 0207/600-3699. www.museumoflondon.org.uk. Free admission, except for temporary exhibits. Mon–Sat 10am–6pm; Sun noon–5:50pm. Tube: St. Paul's.

Conveniently located next to the Museum of London is ⑧ Pizza Express, a branch of one of London's better pizza chains. You'll also find generous servings of well-priced salads, pastas, and delicious desserts. Service is very efficient. 125 Alban Gate, London Wall. ☎ 0207/600-8880. $$ ●

The fairytale Lord Mayor's Coach is the star attraction at the Museum of London.

Kids' London

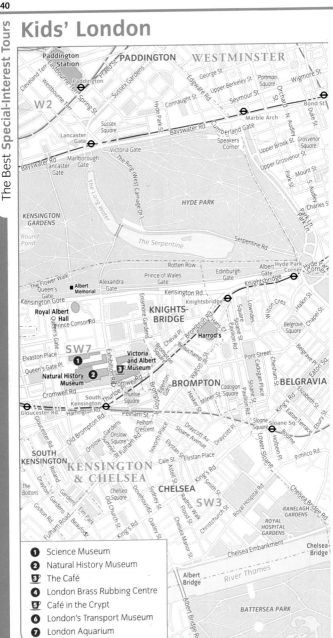

1. Science Museum
2. Natural History Museum
3. The Café
4. London Brass Rubbing Centre
5. Café in the Crypt
6. London's Transport Museum
7. London Aquarium

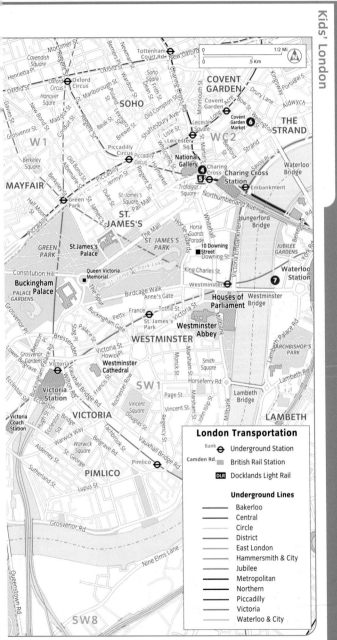

London Transportation

Bank   ⊖   Underground Station

Camden Rd. ▦ British Rail Station

DLR   Docklands Light Rail

Underground Lines

———— Bakerloo
———— Central
———— Circle
———— District
———— East London
———— Hammersmith & City
———— Jubilee
———— Metropolitan
———— Northern
———— Piccadilly
———— Victoria
———— Waterloo & City

London is one of Europe's best playgrounds for kids. Nearly all the city's major museums have developed well-thought-out activities to entertain and inspire kids on weekends and show off the collections to their best advantage. Whether you make it to all the venues on this tour obviously depends on the temperaments and ages of your children. START: **South Kensington Tube Station**

One of the many interactive exhibits at the Science Museum.

1 ★★★ kids **Science Museum.** Designed to appeal to children of all ages, this great institution offers consistently arresting exhibits with fun features, including The Garden, an interactive play area for 3- to 6-year-olds on the Lower Ground Floor. Its seven levels of displays succeed in getting both kids and adults to understand the place of science in everyday life, even as they provide hours of amusement. Highlights include "The Secret of the Home" (cool domestic gadgets), Foucault's Pendulum, the Apollo 10 command module, and an IMAX theater and simulator rides (both of which charge a fee—buy your tickets as soon as you arrive). The gift shop is almost as exciting as the exhibits. ⏱ *2 hr. Come weekdays to avoid weekend throngs. Exhibition Rd.* ☎ *0207/ 942-4454. www.sciencemuseum. org.uk. Free admission, except for special exhibits. Daily 10am–6pm. Tube: South Kensington.*

2 ★★★ kids **Natural History Museum.** This museum's building alone is worth a look. Statues of beasts have been incorporated into its facade; and in the lobby, you'll find charming stained-glass windows. Although not as edgy and modern as the Science Museum next door, this museum is no fossil. Its renovated exhibits include modern dinosaur displays and an interactive rainforest. The gem, mineral, and meteorite exhibits are all top-notch. The old animal dioramas are still around, but the new Darwin Wing (Phase Two of its development will be completed in 2007) has left them in the dust; its highlights include ongoing events with naturalists, photographers, and explorers (not to mention its 28 million insects and 6 million plant specimens). ⏱ *1½ hr. Cromwell Rd., off Exhibition Rd.* ☎ *0207/942-5000. www.nhm.ac.uk. Free admission,*

One of many animal carvings on the façade of the Natural History Museum.

except for temporary exhibits. Daily 10am–6pm. Tube: South Kensington.

3 kids The Café is a renovated cafeteria in the basement of the V&A (p 27) and a good spot to take the kids. It serves hot food (roasts and vegetarian options), deli sandwiches, delicious desserts, and great teatime scones. *Victoria & Albert Museum, Cromwell Rd.* ☎ *0207/942-2000. $*

4 ★★★ kids London Brass Rubbing Centre. Inside the crypt of St. Martin-in-the-Fields are 88 bronze plates of medieval subjects that kids (and adults) can reproduce by rubbing a waxy crayon over a piece of paper affixed to the plate. Admission is free, but rubbings start at £3 for a small drawing (a life-size knight will set you back about £16). Kids love the activity, as it takes no particular skill; and adults will appreciate the classical music playing in the background. The Centre also sells great souvenirs. ⏲ *1 hr. St. Martin-in-the-Fields, Trafalgar Sq.* ☎ *0207/930-9306. Free admission; rubbings from £3. Daily 10am–6:30pm.*

Also in the basement of St. Martin-in-the-Fields Church, **5 ★ Café in the Crypt** is a handy, no-fuss cafe that serves hot lunches, snacks, sweets, and drinks. *St. Martin-in-the-Fields, Trafalgar Sq.* ☎ *0207/839-4342. Tube: Charing Cross. $*

6 ★★★ kids London's Transport Museum. Climb aboard a stagecoach, a double-decker omnibus, or an early underground train at this fascinating museum, where 15 interactive KidZones entertain as they educate. Your family will be given tickets to take around and stamp at each of these zones as you trace the evolution of

London's Transport Museum features lots of family-friendly hands-on exhibits.

London's public transport through photos, old vehicles, models, and more. ⏲ *1½ hr. Covent Garden Piazza.* ☎ *0207/379-6344. www.ltmuseum.co.uk. Admission £5.95 adults, £4.50 seniors, free for kids under 16. Daily 10am–6pm. Tube: Covent Garden.*

7 ★★ kids London Aquarium. You'd expect a bit more for your money at one of Europe's top aquariums, but when it comes down to it, kids adore this place. There's a petting tank of manta rays, a simulated coral reef with seahorses, and appropriately scary shark tanks. Great gift shop for kids. ⏲ *1 hr. County Hall, Westminster Bridge Rd.* ☎ *0207/967-8000. www.london aquarium.co.uk. Admission £8.75 adults, £6.50 seniors, £5.25 kids 3–14, free for kids under 3, £25 family. Daily 10am–6pm. Tube: Westminster.*

Kids love making brass rubbings at St. Martin-in-the-Fields.

Royal London

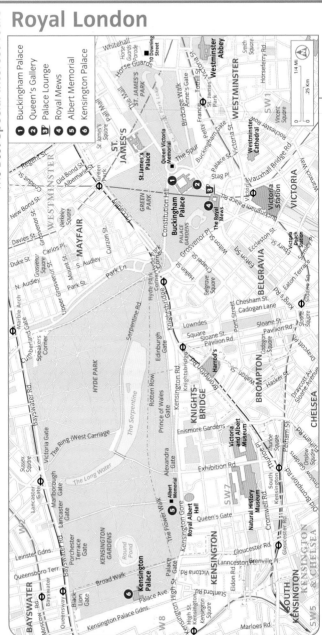

1 Buckingham Palace
2 Queen's Gallery
3 Palace Lounge
4 Royal Mews
5 Albert Memorial
6 Kensington Palace

The justifications for keeping the institution of the English monarchy inevitably come around to the care and feeding of tourists, who can't get enough of the wealth, history, and gossip that define 21st-century royalty. This full-day tour serves up some of the city's royal highlights and offers a glimpse into the London lives of royals past and present. START: **Green Park Tube Station**

A gilded royal insignia on the gates of Buckingham Palace.

❶ ★★ **Buckingham Palace.** The main draw of Queen Elizabeth II's official residence—a magnificent 500-room house that Queen Victoria despaired of ever making livable—is its exclusivity: It's open only in August and September, when the queen is not at home. The palace was originally built for the Duke of Buckingham and sold to King George III (who needed the room for his 15 kids) in 1761. George IV had it remodeled by famed architect John Nash in the 1820s, and the grandiose State Rooms you tour today remain virtually unchanged from his time. As an attraction, the treasure-laden palace has an aloofness that may cause you to question its cost and effort, but it can't be beat for a look at how the Upper Crust live. ⏱ *2 hr. Book the earliest timed tour possible via the website to avoid the worst of the lines. Buckingham Palace Rd.* ☎ *0207/766-7300. www.royal residences.com. Admission (includes self-guided audio tour) £12 adults, £5.50 kids 5–15, £30 family. Aug–Sept, daily 9:30am–4:30pm. Tube: Green Park.*

❷ ★★ **Queen's Gallery.** What used to be a cramped jumble of priceless treasures from the queen's private collection is now an orderly display of paintings, jewelry, furniture, and bibelots of untold value housed in sumptuous Georgian-style surroundings. The exhibits rotate (the queen's holdings include, among other items, 10,000 Old Masters and enough objets d'art to fill several palaces), but whatever is on display will be fabulous. A highlight on my last trip here was an 18th-century solid-silver vanity table. You'll also find the city's best gift shop for royalty-related items, both cheap and dear. ⏱ *1½ hr. Buckingham Gate.* ☎ *0207/766-7301. www.royal residences.com. Timed tickets necessary in summer. Admission £7.50 adults, £6 seniors, £4 kids 5–16, free for kids under 5. Daily 10am–4:30pm. Tube: Green Park.*

A Fabergé egg on display at the Queen's Gallery.

Overlooking the entrance to the Royal Mews is the **3 Palace Lounge,** an atmospheric spot to grab a cup of tea or a tasty light meal. Lucky visitors may get a glimpse of deliveries being made to Buckingham Palace in old-fashioned wagons. *In the Rubens at the Palace, 39 Buckingham Palace Rd.* ☎ *0207/834-6600. $$*

4 ★ **kids Royal Mews.** This oddly affecting royal experience is a great diversion on its own, or if you're waiting for your timed entry to Buckingham Palace or the Queen's Gallery. Even if you're not into horses, you'll be fascinated by this peek into the lives of the queen's privileged equines. The stalls at this working stable are roomy, the tack is pristine, and the ceremonial carriages (including the ornate Gold State Coach and the coach Princess Diana rode to her wedding to Prince Charles) are eye-popping. A small exhibit tells you about the role the queen's horses have played in the past and present; old sepia-toned pictures show various royals and their four-footed friends. ⏱ *45 min. Buckingham Gate.* ☎ *0207/766-7301. www.royalresidences.com. Admission £5.50 adults, £4.50 seniors, £3 kids 5–16. Oct–July, Mon–Thurs*

You can visit the queen's horses and carriages at the Royal Mews.

The Albert Memorial, Queen Victoria's elaborate shrine to her husband.

noon–4pm; Aug–Sept, Mon–Thurs 10:30am–5pm. Tube: Green Park.

5 ★ **kids Albert Memorial.** An inconsolable Queen Victoria spent an obscene amount of public money on this 55m-tall (180-ft.) shrine to her husband Albert, who died of typhoid fever in 1861. The project (completed in 1876) didn't go down too well with many of her ministers, but Victoria was not a woman to whom one said no. The excessively ornate mass of gilt, marble, statuary, and mosaics set in Kensington Gardens was restored (to the tune of millions of pounds) in the 1990s, and now stands in all its dubious glory across the street from the equally fabulous (and somewhat more useful) Albert Hall. That book Albert is holding is a catalogue from the Great Exhibition of which he was patron, and which formed the basis for the great museums of South Kensington (which was once called Albertropolis). ⏱ *30 min. Kensington Gardens (west of Exhibition Rd.). Free admission. Daily dawn to dusk. Tube: Kensington High St.*

6 ★★ **kids** **Kensington Palace.** Once the 17th-century country refuge of monarchs William III and Mary II, this former home of Princess Diana is more satisfying to visit than Buckingham Palace (and it's open year-round). The palace is smaller, has more personality, and is more manageable to visit than Buckingham, with a number of pleasing architectural details that span the years from Jacobean England to the early 19th century.

Kensington Palace Highlights

William III's Small Bedchamber is now called the **6A** ★★ **18th-Century Dress Rooms,** housing samples of the flamboyant clothing worn by the ladies and gentlemen of the royal court from 1750 to 1770. They're also home to the Royal Ceremonial Dress Collection, which features gowns worn by the queen and the late Princess Diana. The **6B** ★ **King's Grand Staircase** has a magnificent wrought-iron balustrade; its elaborate 16th-century-style Italianate murals on the walls and ceiling were commissioned by George I in 1725. The lavishly decorated **6C** **Cupola Room** features elaborately carved chandeliers, a breathtaking gilt clock, and a magnificent painted ceiling. **6D** **Queen Victoria's Bedroom,** hung with artwork commissioned by Victoria and Albert, is where the young princess and her mother slept until the teenager ascended the throne in 1837. **6E** **Queen Mary's Bedchamber** was likely the room where Mary II died of smallpox in 1694; the bed, however, probably belonged to James II.

🕐 *2 hr. The Broad Walk, Kensington Gardens.* ☎ *0207/937-9561. www.hrp.org.uk. Admission (includes self-guided audio tour) £11 adults, £8.20 seniors, £7 kids 5–15, free for kids under 5. Daily 10am–5pm. Tube: Kensington High St.*

A gown worn by the late Princess Diana on display at Kensington Palace.

Hampton Court Palace

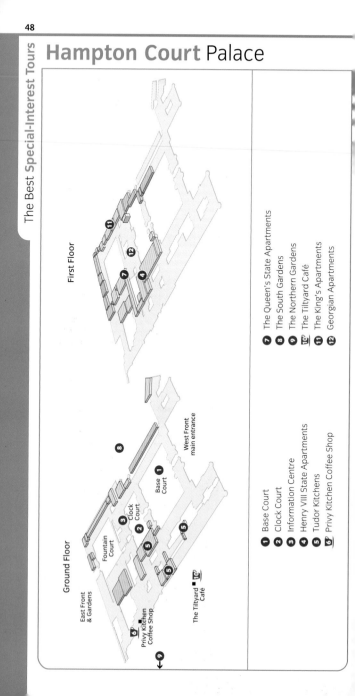

First Floor

Ground Floor

East Front
& Gardens

Fountain
Court

Clock
Court

Base
Court

West Front
main entrance

Privy Kitchen
Coffee Shop

The Tiltyard
Café

① Base Court
② Clock Court
③ Information Centre
④ Henry VIII State Apartments
⑤ Tudor Kitchens
⑥ Privy Kitchen Coffee Shop

⑦ The Queen's State Apartments
⑧ The South Gardens
⑨ The Northern Gardens
⑩ The Tiltyard Café
⑪ The King's Apartments
⑫ Georgian Apartments

This Tudor masterpiece was built by Cardinal Thomas Wolsey in 1514, only to be snatched up by Henry VIII (1509–1547). It served as a royal residence from 1528 to 1737, and few places in England exude as much historic atmosphere. Tread the same paths as Elizabeth I (1558–1603), William III (1689–1702), and George II (1727–1760) as you learn about life at court through the centuries. START: **Hampton Court Station**

1 Base Court. Monarchs arrived at Hampton Court via the Thames and entered through the gardens, but visitors today pass through a gatehouse built by Henry VIII for the common folk, and into the Tudor-style courtyard, which is almost exactly as it was when Cardinal Wolsey first built it in 1515. Be sure to examine the turrets surrounding the courtyard, which sport the insignia of Henry VIII and Elizabeth I (who both resided here), as well as numerous carved heads of Roman emperors. ⏱ *10 min.*

2 ★★ Clock Court. From the Base Court, pass through the Anne Boleyn Gatehouse (built in the 19th century, long after the beheaded queen's death) and into the Clock Court, which encompasses several architectural styles, ranging from Tudor (the north side) to 18th-century

Hampton Court's famous Astronomical Clock.

A costumed-guided tour of Hampton Court is wonderful for both kids and adults.

Gothic (the east side). The major attraction is the elaborate Astronomical Clock, built for Henry VIII (note the sun revolving around the earth—the clock was built before Galileo and Copernicus debunked that myth). ⏱ *15 min.*

3 ★★★ kids Book a Guided Tour. Stop in at the Information Centre inside the baroque colonnade on the south side of the Clock Court and book a spot on one of the day's costumed-guided tours (included with your admission fee). The guides here are knowledgeable and entertaining, and dispense juicy historical tidbits. Kids especially enjoy the experience. You must book in person; do so as soon as you get to the palace, as space on these tours is limited. If you have a choice, opt for the tour of the Henry VIII State Apartments or the King's Apartments. Self-guided palace audio tours are also available (and free). ⏱ *10 min.*

④ ★★★ **Henry VIII State Apartments.** Even though Sir Christopher Wren modified some of them, these rooms represent the best examples of Tudor style in England. Don't miss the elaborately gilded ceiling of the **Chapel Royal,** a still-functioning church where Henry was informed of the "misconduct" of his adulterous fifth wife, Catherine Howard, and later married wife number six, Catherine Parr. Right off the chapel is the **Haunted Gallery,** where Howard's ghost reportedly still pleads for her life. The **Watching Chamber,** where senior courtiers would dine, is the only one of Henry VIII's many English estate rooms in something close to its original form (the fireplace and stained glass are not originals). Also impressive is the **Great Hall,** with a set of tapestries (real gold and silver thread) that cost Henry as much as his naval fleet. ⏱ *45 min.*

⑤ ★★ **Tudor Kitchens.** At its peak, Hampton Court's kitchen staff catered two meals a day to a household of 800. Once the palace lost its popularity with the royal set, the 50-room kitchens were converted into apartments. They were restored in

The Tudor kitchens, restored to look as they did during the reign of Henry VIII.

1991. The enormity of the labor needed to feed the household here is best experienced in the appropriately named **Great Kitchens.** In a small hatchway just outside them are the intriguing **Dressers,** where servants would "dress" and garnish platters sent up to the senior courtiers (check out the marzipan on the table—it's being painted with real gold). ⏱ *45 min.*

The atmospheric ⑥ ★ **kids** **Privy Kitchen Coffee Shop** offers a Tudor-style atmosphere (think wooden tables and 16th-century-style chandeliers) along with decent pastries, light lunches, and afternoon tea. $

⑦ ★ **The Queen's State Apartments.** The rooms in this section of the palace generally appear as they were when Queen Caroline, wife of George II, from 1716 to 1737. As you climb the frescoed **Staircase,** note Caroline's and George's monograms in the corners of the ceiling. Most impressive is the ornate **State Bedchamber,** one of the only rooms with all of its original furnishings and tapestries (including the heavily draped 18th-century bed). The **Gallery** was actually built for Queen Mary II (1689–84), and displays top-notch pieces of Delftware and Chinese ceramics. ⏱ *25 min.*

The Chapel Royal is renowned for its gilt ceiling.

8 ★★★ **The South Gardens.** The palace's most impressive gardens are home to William III's **Privy Garden,** with its elaborate baroque ironwork screen; the box-hedged **Knot Garden,** which resembles a traditional Tudor garden; and the lovely sunken **Pond Gardens,** which were originally ponds where the palace's fish were kept before delivery to the kitchens. Don't skip Mantegna's *Triumph of Caesar,* a series of nine paintings housed in the Lower Orangery (a re-creation of Palace San Sebastiano in Mantua), which are among the most important works of the Italian Renaissance. ⏱ 40 min.

The king's Privy Garden in full bloom.

9 ★★ **kids The Northern Gardens.** Renowned for their spring bulbs, the Northern Gardens are also where you'll find the palace's famous **Hedge Maze,** whose labyrinthine paths cover nearly a half-mile. Planted in 1702, the maze has trapped many a visitor in its clutches. When you do escape, stroll the adjacent **Tiltyard,** where you'll find several smaller gardens, as well as the only surviving tiltyard tower (used to seat spectators at tournaments) built by Henry VIII. ⏱ 30–45 min.

10 ★ **The Tiltyard Café** offers well-priced sandwiches, salads, afternoon teas, and light meals in a slightly upscale setting. If the weather's good, try to sit on the outdoor terrace. You can also picnic on the grass around the cafe, or on the benches in the Clock Court. $

11 ★★★ **The King's Apartments.** These baroque rooms (among the finest of their kind) were designed by Christopher Wren for William III (1689–1702), who did more to shape the palace than any other monarch, though he died shortly after moving in. The apartments were badly damaged in a 1986 fire (you can still see scorch marks on the ceiling in the **Privy Chamber**), but have been fully restored. All the rooms in this wing are impressive, but a few have notable features. The **Guard Chamber** features a spectacular collection of nearly 3,000 weapons; the **Presence Chamber** has an exquisite rock-crystal chandelier; the **Private Dining Room** has a reproduction of the king's gold-plated dining service (strictly for show); and the **Great Bedchamber** (ceremonial only—the king slept elsewhere) is loaded with gilded furniture, priceless tapestries, and a magnificent red-velvet canopy bed. ⏱ 1 hr.

Lose yourself in the tall greenery of the Hedge Maze.

The Queen's Bedchamber is one of the highlights of the Georgian Rooms.

⑫ ★★ Georgian Apartments.
The private apartments of George II and Queen Caroline still look as they did in 1737, when Caroline died and the royal court left the palace behind forever. The **Presence Chamber** of the 10-year-old Duke of Cumberland (the king's second son) is the only room at the palace that's fully paneled, gilded, and painted. Only a portion of the ceiling of the **Wolsey Closet** is from the Tudor era, though the ceiling is decorated in the Renaissance style. The state bed in the **Queen's Bedchamber** is a reproduction. If the king and queen wanted to sleep together in privacy (which was no mean feat for the royal couple), it was to this room they retired, thanks to a rather sophisticated door lock. ⏲ *45 min.* ●

Practical Matters

Hampton Court Palace (☎ 0870/752-7777; www.hrp.org.uk) is located in Molsey, Surrey, 21km (13 miles) west of London. Take a train out of London's Waterloo Station to Hampton Court Station; when you exit the station, turn right and follow the signs to the palace, a 10-minute walk away.

Admission to the palace and gardens costs £12 adults, £7.70 kids 5 to 16, £35 family (two adults, three kids). To avoid waiting in lines, and to obtain a £1 discount per ticket, book your tickets on the website (there is a £3 service fee per order—not per ticket). Visa and Mastercard are accepted. Tickets are mailed to you or may be picked up at the Prepaid Ticket kiosk on the right side as you face the main ticket booth. The admission fee also includes a free self-guided audio tour; inquire at the Information Centre inside the Clock Court (see bullet ❸).

The palace is open daily 10am to 6pm from April to October (the best time to visit); daily 10am to 4:30pm from November to March. The gardens are open 7am until dusk. Closed December 24, 25, and 26. Arrive at opening time to beat the crowds.

The West Front entrance at Hampton Court Palace.

Chelsea

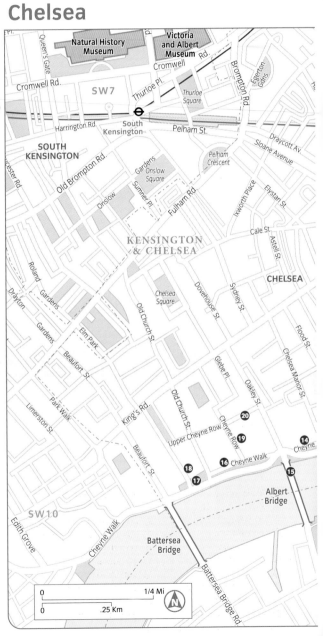

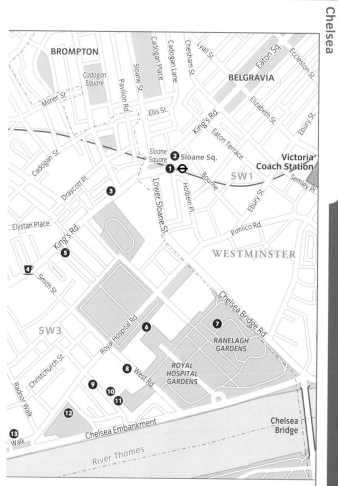

1. Sloane Square
2. Royal Court Theatre
3. King's Road
4. Chelsea Kitchen
5. Royal Avenue
6. Chelsea Royal Hospital
7. Ranelagh Gardens
8. National Army Museum
9. Oscar Wilde's Home
10. Augustus John's Studio
11. John Singer Sargent's Home
12. Chelsea Physic Garden
13. George Eliot's Home
14. Dante Gabriel Rossetti's Home
15. Albert Bridge
16. Carlyle Mansions
17. Statue of Sir Thomas More
18. Chelsea Old Church
19. Thomas Carlyle's House
20. Leigh Hunt's Home

Since the 16th century, when Henry VIII and Thomas More built country manors on its bucolic Thames riverbanks, Chelsea has had a long tradition of eccentricity, aristocracy, and artisanship. Home to some of the most picturesque buildings in London, this posh district is one of my favorite spots for a stroll. Keep an eye peeled for blue plaques affixed to the local houses; they tell the story of the many leading figures of English culture who once called this neighborhood home. START: **Sloane Square Tube Station**

1 ★★ **Sloane Square.** Physician Sir Hans Sloane (1660–1753), who helped found the British Museum and at one point owned most of Chelsea, is the namesake of this attractive square. In addition to his educational and medical achievements, Sloane discovered the chocolate recipe that became the basis of the Cadbury empire. *Intersection of Sloane St. and King's Rd.*

2 ★★ **Royal Court Theatre.** This restored theater, originally built in 1888, is famous for showcasing playwrights such as George Bernard Shaw, John Osborne, and Harold Pinter. Nowadays, the work of today's most promising dramatists is performed on the two stages. *A few steps to the right of the Sloane Sq. Tube exit.* ☎ *0207/565-5000. www.royalcourttheatre.com.*

3 ★★★ **King's Road.** Chelsea's main road was once an exclusive royal passage used by Charles II to go from Whitehall to Hampton Court. It was also a favorite route of highwaymen looking to "liberate" some royal goods. An echo of these King's Road robbers can

King's Road, Chelsea's major thoroughfare, is loaded with ritzy shops.

be found in the extortionate prices of the chi-chi stores that now line this shopping-focused thoroughfare. The area is a favorite of the young and free-spending members of London's upper social strata. *Runs from Sloane Sq. southwest to Putney Bridge.*

Known for its casual and congenial atmosphere, **4** ★ **Chelsea Kitchen** has been a local favorite since it opened in 1961. The basic British food may not be the best in London, but the soups and fish-and-chips are tasty, the prices are very reasonable, and it stays open until 11:30pm. *98 King's Rd.* ☎ *0207/589-1330. $*

Fountain in Sloane Square.

5 ★ **Royal Avenue.** This small, picturesque road was intended to extend all the way from nearby Chelsea Royal Hospital to Kensington Palace when it was laid out in 1682 by Sir Christopher Wren, but construction was cut short upon the death of its commissioner, Charles II. *Between St. Leonard's Terrace and King's Rd.*

6 ★★★ **Chelsea Royal Hospital.** This Christopher Wren masterpiece, commissioned by Charles II in 1692 as a retirement estate for injured and old soldiers, is home to 400-plus pensioners who still dress in traditional uniforms and offer informative tours of the historic grounds and chapel. It's the site of Chelsea's Flower Show, held every May since 1912. *Royal Hospital Rd.* ☎ *0207/881-0161. Free admission. Guided tours by prior arrangement only. Mon–Sat 10am–noon, 2–4pm; Sun 2–4pm. Church services open to public, Sun 10:30am.*

7 ★★ **Ranelagh Gardens.** Once centered about a large rotunda (demolished in 1805), these gardens (some of the prettiest in London)

A plaque marks the site of Oscar Wilde's Chelsea home.

were a favorite of 18th-century socialites who were occasionally entertained here by a young Mozart. *At Chelsea Royal Hospital. Free admission. Mon–Sat 10am–noon, 2–4pm; Sun 2–4pm.*

8 ★★ **National Army Museum.** Home of the Duke of Wellington's shaving mirror and Florence Nightingale's lamp, this museum follows the history of Britain's fighting forces from the Middle Ages to the present. *Royal Hospital Rd.* ☎ *0207/730-0717. www.national-army-museum.ac.uk. Free admission. Daily 10am–5:30pm.*

9 ★★ **Oscar Wilde's Home.** The eccentricities of Oscar and his wife Constance (they lived here from 1885 until 1895) were well known to neighbors, who would often see them on the street dressed in velvet (him) and a huge Gainsborough hat (her). Street boys would shout, "'Ere comes 'Amlet and Ophelia!" The house is not open to the public. *34 Tite St.*

10 ★ **Augustus John's Studio.** A renowned Welsh painter (1878–1961), John was one of Chelsea's most illustrious artists. His insightful portraits and landscapes made him famous, while his bohemian lifestyle and love affairs (including one with the mother of James Bond–creator Ian Fleming) earned him notoriety. *33 Tite St.*

One of Chelsea Royal Hospital's pensioners.

Gardeners will delight in Chelsea Physic Garden's bounty of herbs and plants.

⓫ ★★ John Singer Sargent's Home. The renowned American portraitist of the high and mighty lived and worked at this address (the former abode of the equally famous artist James McNeill Whistler) from 1901 until his death in 1925. *31 Tite St.*

⓬ ★★ Chelsea Physic Garden. This garden was established in 1673 by the Apothecaries' Company to cultivate medicinal plants and herbs. Cotton seeds from the garden were sent to America in 1732, and slavery became their eventual harvest. *66 Royal Hospital Rd.* ☎ *0207/352-5646. www. chelseaphysicgarden.co.uk. Admission £5 adults, £3 kids 5–15. Apr to late Oct: Wed noon–5pm, Sun 2–6pm. Check website for special opening times.*

⓭ ★ George Eliot's Home. The famous Victorian novelist, born Mary Ann Evans in 1819, moved into this house with her new and much younger husband, John Cross, only a few months before her death in December 1880. *4 Cheyne Walk.*

⓮ ★ Dante Gabriel Rossetti's Home. The eccentric pre-Raphaelite poet and painter (1828–82) moved here in 1862 after the death of his wife. He kept a menagerie of many exotic animals, including kangaroos, a white bull, peacocks, and a wombat that inspired his friend, Lewis Carroll, to create the Dormouse in *Alice In Wonderland. 16 Cheyne Walk.*

⓯ ★★★ Albert Bridge. Designed by R. M. Ordish, this picturesque suspension bridge linking Battersea and Chelsea was completed in 1873. Conservationists kept the bridge from destruction in the 1950s. In 1973, the cast-iron structure had new supports installed so it could cope with the rigors of modern traffic. The sight of seagulls and sparrows wheeling above the span is part of its considerable charm.

⓰ ★ Carlyle Mansions. Henry James (1843–1916), the great American novelist *(Portrait of a Lady)*, was sick in bed inside his river-view flat when he was honored for his work (and for taking British citizenship) with the Order of the British Empire. Only a few weeks later, the writer drew his last breath here in this apartment complex. *Cheyne Walk.*

The Albert Bridge spans the Thames, linking Battersea with Chelsea.

This statue of Sir Thomas More stands just outside Chelsea Old Church.

has since been rebuilt and restored. Sir Thomas More worshipped here (he built the South Chapel in 1528), and it was also the setting of Henry VIII's secret marriage to third wife Jane Seymour in 1536. *64 Cheyne Walk.* ☎ *0207/795-1019. www. chelseaoldchurch.org.uk.*

⑲ ★★★ Thomas Carlyle's House. The famous Scottish historian (1795–1881) and his wife, Jane, entertained friends Dickens and Chopin in this remarkably well-preserved Victorian home. It was here that the "Sage of Chelsea" finished his important *History of the French Revolution. 24 Cheyne Row.* ☎ *0207/352-7087. www. nationaltrust.org.uk. Admission £3.70 adults, £1.80 kids 5–16. Apr–Oct, Wed–Fri 2–5pm, Sat–Sun 11am–5pm.*

⑳ ★ Leigh Hunt's Home. From 1833 to 1840, the noted poet and essayist (a friend of Byron and Keats) lived here, and was well known for pestering neighbors for loans. His wife infuriated Jane Carlyle with her incessant borrowing of household items. *22 Upper Cheyne Row.*

The Victorian home of historian Thomas Carlyle has been remarkably preserved.

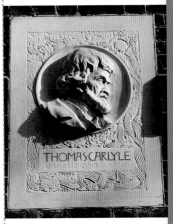

⑰ ★★ Statue of Sir Thomas More.
Despite his long friendship with Henry VIII, Lord Chancellor Thomas More (1478–1535) refused to accept Henry as head of the Church of England after the king's notorious break with the Roman Catholic Church. More paid for his religious convictions with his life—he was tried and subsequently beheaded for treason in 1535. In 1935, the Roman Catholic Church canonized him as Saint Thomas More, the patron saint of lawyers and politicians. *Old Church St.*

⑱ ★★ Chelsea Old Church.
A church has stood on this site since 1157. Though the structure suffered serious damage during the Blitz, it

Hampstead

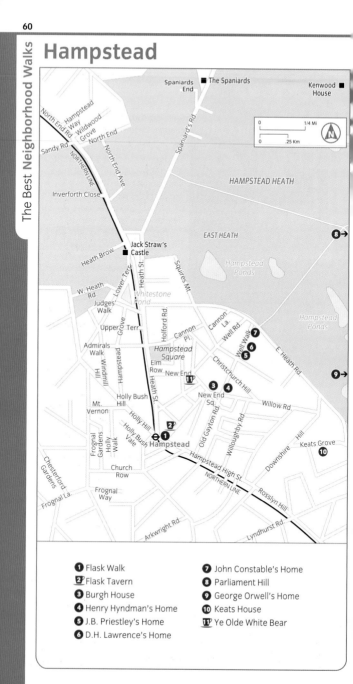

Spaniards End   ■ The Spaniards

Kenwood House ■

North End Rd.

Hampstead Way

Wildwood Grove

North End

Sandy Rd.

NORTHERN LINE

North End Ave.

Spaniard's Rd.

HAMPSTEAD HEATH

0   1/4 Mi

0   .25 Km

Inverforth Close

Heath Brow

EAST HEATH

8 →

W. Heath Rd.

Jack Straw's Castle ■

Heath St.

Squires Mt.

Hampstead Ponds

Judges' Walk

Lower Terr.

Whitestone Pond

Upper Terr.

Grove

Holford Rd.

Cannon Pl.

Cannon La.

Well Rd.

Well Walk

7

Hampstead Ponds

Admirals Walk

Hampstead

Elm Row

Hampstead Square

New End

Christchurch Hill

6
5

E. Heath Rd.

Windmill Hill

Heath St.

11

3 **4**

New End Sq.

9 →

Mt. Vernon

Holly Bush Hill

Holly Hill

Old Gayton Rd.

Willoughby Rd.

Willow Rd.

Frognal Gardens

Holly Walk

Holly Bush Vale

2

Downshire Hill

Keats Grove

Church Row

1

Hampstead ⊖

Hampstead High St.

10

Chesterford Gardens

NORTHERN LINE

Rosslyn Hill

Frognal La.

Frognal Way

Arkwright Rd.

Lyndhurst Rd.

1 Flask Walk
2 Flask Tavern
3 Burgh House
4 Henry Hyndman's Home
5 J.B. Priestley's Home
6 D.H. Lawrence's Home

7 John Constable's Home
8 Parliament Hill
9 George Orwell's Home
10 Keats House
11 Ye Olde White Bear

Hampstead first became popular for its fresh air and salubrious waters during the Great Plague of 1660, when well-to-do Londoners bolted from their infected neighborhoods to escape the contagion before they were quarantined with the dying. Today, this village is still a charming refuge, known for its historical buildings, fun shops, and bracing proximity to the Heath, 324 hectares (800 acres) of controlled wilderness and far-reaching views. Come here for a look at a kinder, gentler London. START: **Hampstead Tube Station**

❶ ★ **Flask Walk.** Now a street of expensive homes and chi-chi shops, Flask Walk was the site of early 18th-century fairs and also home to year-round establishments for drinking and gambling—all built to entertain the crush of Londoners escaping the fetid city streets for Hampstead's fresh air. The street was named for a now-defunct tavern that bottled the village's pure water and sold it throughout London.

Explore the local history of Hampstead at Burgh House.

The three-room ❷ ★★ **Flask Tavern,** a Victorian pub built in 1874 on the site of the old Thatched House Pub, is cozy in the winter thanks to its cast-iron fireplace, and offers a few outdoor tables in good weather. It serves reliable pub grub, and is worth visiting for its appealing atmosphere. *14 Flask Walk.* ☎ *0207/435-4580. MC, V. $$*

❸ ★ **Burgh House.** Built in 1704, this restored Queen Anne structure, the former home of spa physician Dr. William Gibbon, now houses a museum that specializes in the local history of Hampstead and features a permanent exhibit on the painter John Constable, who lived nearby. *New End Sq.* ☎ *0207/431-0144. www.burghhouse.org.uk. Free admission. Wed–Sun noon–5pm.*

Flask Walk in the village of Hampstead.

④ ★ Henry Hyndman's Home.
A journalist, politician, and public speaker, Hyndman (1842–1921) founded the Social Democratic Federation, England's first socialist party, in 1881. He lived in this house until his death in 1921. *13 Well Walk.*

⑤ ★ J. B. Priestley's Home.
One of England's most prolific men of letters, Priestley (1894–1984) was an essayist, playwright, biographer, historian, and social commentator who refused a knighthood and peerage. He lived in this Queen Anne–style house from 1929 to 1931. *28 Well Walk.*

⑥ ★★ D. H. Lawrence's Home.
During World War I, Lawrence (1885–1930) made his home here after being kicked out of Cornwall when his wife was unjustly accused of being a German spy. He left in 1919 for Italy, where he wrote his most famous novel, *Lady Chatterley's Lover,* in 1928. The book was banned in England on charges of indecency and wasn't published there uncensored until 1960. *32 Well Walk.*

Stand atop Parliament Hill for some of the loveliest views of London.

The greenery of Hampstead Heath has inspired many a writer and artist.

⑦ ★★ John Constable's Home. The well-known British landscape painter and portraitist resided here from 1827 until his death in 1837. It was in his many studies of nearby Hampstead Heath that Constable mastered the depiction of weather in landscapes, tirelessly painting the same scene under different climatic conditions. *40 Well Walk.*

⑧ ★★★ Parliament Hill. Guy Fawkes and his co-conspirators in the 1605 Gunpowder Plot to blow up Parliament planned to view the aftermath of their handiwork from this vantage point. It's the best place to watch the fireworks staged every November 5 to commemorate the plot. A map on the site identifies the buildings in the distance. *Inside Hampstead Heath.*

⑨ ★★ George Orwell's Home.
The author of *Animal Farm, 1984,* and the classic book on London, *Down and Out in Paris and London,* wrote the satirical *Keep the Aspidistra Flying* in a back room on the second floor of this house. He lived here for only 6 months in 1936 while working part-time at Booklover's Corner, a small bookshop on South End Green (it's now a pizza shop). *77 Parliament Hill St.*

❿ ★★★ **Keats House.** It was in this house (built by combining two Regency cottages), in 1819, that Keats wrote his famous *Ode to a Nightingale, Ode on a Grecian Urn,* and *Ode to Psyche.* It was also while living here that Keats fell in love with next-door neighbor Fanny Brawne, his eventual fiancée (and the muse behind many of his best works). The Romantic poet lived in this house from 1818 until 1820, when he traveled to Italy, where he died of tuberculosis only a few months later. The house is now a museum that pays tribute to the short life of this great poet. *Keats Grove.* ☎ *0207/435-2062. http://www.cityoflondon.gov.uk/ keats. Adults £3, free for kids under 16. Mid-Apr to Oct, Tues–Sun noon–5pm; Nov–Mar, Tues–Sun noon–4pm.*

The poet John Keats wrote his famous Ode on a Grecian Urn while living in this Hampstead house.

With dark woodcarvings, fine furniture, and photos of the area's celebs on the walls, ⓫ ★★ **Ye Olde White Bear** manages to project the atmosphere of a country village pub, even though it serves sophisticated Londoners and features urban prices. *Corner of Well Rd. and New End Rd.* ☎ *0207/435-3758. MC, V. $*

The Loos of London

One of London's greatest public conveniences is the ubiquity of public lavatories, making the city far friendlier to the strolling visitor than, say, New York. Public restrooms are usually quite clean and stocked with toilet paper. These oases for the visitor used to cost 1 pence, hence the local euphemism for nature's call, "Spending a penny." Today, you've got to spend 20 pence, at either the old-fashioned tiled below-ground Mens or Ladies rooms, or the free-standing metal kiosks that get a complete hose-down and cleaning automatically after each use. Have a 20-pence coin handy at all times, but if you're stuck, you can usually find a free loo at a public library, park, or museum, and you can thank globalization for the restrooms at Starbucks or McDonald's. In a pinch, you can also try a pub or restaurant, though I'd buy a little something to become a customer first. You could try a department store, too.

Mayfair

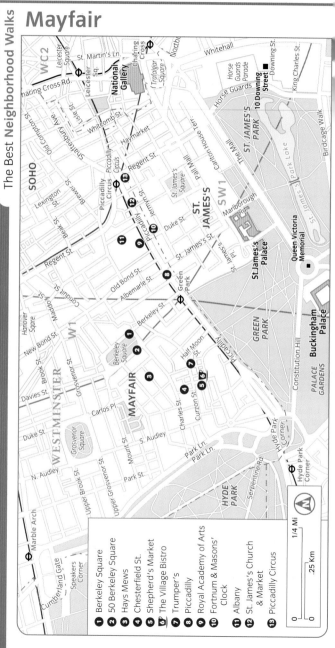

0 ____ 1/4 Mi
0 ____ .25 Km

For over three centuries, Mayfair has been an exclusive neighborhood of the aristocracy, who used to live in grand style inside elegant mansions run by armies of servants. Most of these urban palaces have been destroyed over the years, but enough survive to make a walk through Mayfair a fascinating glimpse into how London's rich lived—and often still live. This walk focuses on the southern part of Mayfair. START: **Green Park Tube Station**

1 ★ **Berkeley Square.** Immortalized in song and associated with nightingales (nowhere to be found today), this square was once the most aristocratic spot in London. Notables who've called the square home include Prime Ministers Winston Churchill (who lived at No. 48 as a boy) and George Canning (who resided briefly at No. 50, see bullet **2**). Its modern east side, loaded with undistinguished office buildings, doesn't bear looking at. Keep your eyes on the lovely old houses on the west side (Lansdowne House on the southwest corner was designed by famed Scottish architect Robert Adam). And check out the maplelike plane trees that surround the square; they were planted in 1789 and are among the oldest in the city.

2 ★★ **50 Berkeley Square.** This Georgian-style building (now home to a respectable bookshop) was known as the "most haunted house in London" in the 19th century, when sightings of a bewigged man and sounds of an unearthly nature kept the house untenanted. Though strange happenings here have been reported as recently as 2001, the worst of the haunting seems to have taken place in Victorian days, when an evil presence in what was known as the "haunted room" so terrified a visitor, he threw himself out the window and was impaled on the railings below.

3 ★ **Hays Mews.** There were once mews—garages with carriages and horses on the lower floor, and

Berkeley Square's west side is home to several picturesque town houses.

living quarters for the groom and coachmen upstairs—like this one found throughout London. Today, most mews have been converted into expensive homes, but some lucky owners still use them for their cars. *To the left of the Coach & Horses Pub on Hays Mews.*

4 ★★ **Chesterfield Street.** This is the least altered Georgian street in Mayfair and a great place to soak up the neighborhood's atmosphere. Its former inhabitants include historians Edward Gibbon and Edmund Burke. As you stroll along its sidewalks, you'll see plaques identifying the former homes of Regency dandy Beau Brummel and writer Somerset Maugham.

5 ★★★ **Shepherd's Market.** In the mid–18th century, developer Edward Shepherd bought the land on which the riotous May Fair (the neighborhood's namesake) took place each spring. Subsequent development put an end to that often-outlawed orgy. The result was much what you see now: charming yet humble buildings from the days when the market was the hub of the servant classes in Mayfair. Where once you would find useful emporia selling meat and groceries, today you'll find upscale chocolate shops and jewelry stores.

Housed in a building dating back to 1741, friendly and unfussy **6** ★★ **The Village Bistro** is an unpretentious diner that serves up all-day breakfasts, great sandwiches, good cappuccino, and very un-Mayfair prices. It's a real treat in this almost too-tony area. *Shepherd's Market.* ☎ *0207/499-4592.* $

7 ★★★ **Trumper's.** Where else can you get a shave with a straight-razor and shaving brush these days? This English institution opened in 1875, and is so authentically old-fashioned that you half expect to be told not to touch anything. Even if you don't need a shave or toiletries, do have a look at this wonderful shop. *9 Curzon St.* ☎ *0207/499-1850. www.trumpers.com.*

8 ★★ **Piccadilly.** The name Piccadilly is said to have come from the word "picadil," a stiff collar manufactured by a tailor of the early 17th century who bought a great parcel of land on which he built a grand home. Lest the upstart forget his humble beginnings, it was sneeringly referred to as "Piccadilly Hall." In the 18th and 19th centuries, many great mansions were built along the street facing Green Park.

Head east on Piccadilly, so you can admire the elaborate gates surrounding Green Park and the carved classical-style heads on the Parisian-inspired facade of the Ritz hotel.

9 ★★★ **Royal Academy of Arts.** Burlington House, built in the 1660s, was a magnificent estate purchased by the government in 1854 to house England's oldest arts society. The Royal Academy mounts popular exhibitions in this small but lovely space. The permanent collection includes one of only four Michelangelo sculptures found outside of Italy. *Burlington House, Piccadilly.* ☎ *0207/300-8000. www.royalacademy.org.uk.*

10 ★★★ **Fortnum & Masons' Clock.** Try to time your arrival here to the hour, so you can see Fortnum & Mason's wonderful glockenspiel clock do its thing. Two liveried

Carved classical heads mark the façade of the Ritz hotel on Piccadilly, a street loaded with interesting architectural styles and features.

Piccadilly Circus, located in the heart of Mayfair, is always hopping with activity.

prime Piccadilly patch home. *At Albany Court off Piccadilly.*

⑫ ★★★ **St. James's Church & Market.** This unprepossessing redbrick church is one of Christopher Wren's simplest, said by Charles Dickens to be "not one of the master's happiest efforts." The poet William Blake was baptized here, as was William Pitt, the first earl of Chatham, who became England's youngest prime minister at age 24. You are welcome to enter and sit in its quiet interior, or enjoy the free (donations gladly accepted) lunchtime recitals. There's a market in the forecourt Tuesday through Saturday, featuring crafts, collectibles, and antiques. *197 Piccadilly.* ☎ *0207/381-0441.* · *www.sjpconcerts.org.*

⑬ ★★ **Piccadilly Circus.** London's answer to New York's Times Square was the first place in the city to sport electrical signage, and it still dazzles the eye at night. The word circus refers to a circular juncture at an intersection of streets, and the plaza was built in 1819 to connect two of London's major shopping streets: Regent Street and Piccadilly. The statue of Eros on the central island of Piccadilly Circus is a favorite meeting place and hangout. Officially, it's called the Shaftesbury Memorial Fountain, designed in 1893 by Alfred Gilbert in memory of the seventh earl of Shaftesbury, a venerable Victorian philanthropist. It was supposed to be a statue of The Angel of Christian Charity, but has always been known as Eros.

The Statue of Eros on the central island of Piccadilly Circus.

mechanical figures (representing messieurs Fortnum and Mason) emerge from the 4-ton contraption and nod politely as the clock marks the hour with 18th-century music. The best vantage point is from the traffic island in the middle of the street. *181 Piccadilly.*

⑪ ★★ **Albany.** Built in the 1770s by architect William Chambers for Lord Melbourne, this grand Georgian building was turned into a residence for gentlemen in 1802. Since then, many poets (Lord Byron), authors (Graham Greene), and playwrights have all called this

Whitehall

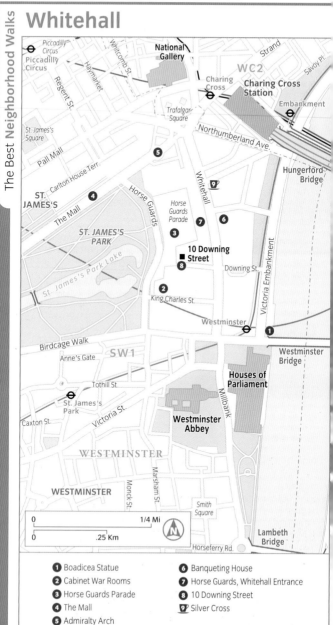

1 Boadicea Statue
2 Cabinet War Rooms
3 Horse Guards Parade
4 The Mall
5 Admiralty Arch
6 Banqueting House
7 Horse Guards, Whitehall Entrance
8 10 Downing Street
📺 Silver Cross

Once the site of the vast Palace of Whitehall—London's chief royal residence from 1530 to 1698—this area is now a dignified neighborhood of government buildings whose elaborate architecture confers a certain beauty to the business of bureaucracy. If London can be said to have a political center, then Whitehall is it. This walk works best in the morning; try to time your arrival at Horse Guards Parade at 11am to see the Changing of the Guard. START: **Westminster Tube Station**

1 ★★ **Boadicea Statue.** A tall and ferocious queen of the Iceni tribe of East Anglia, Boadicea waged battle against Britain's 1st-century Roman invaders, nailing captured soldiers to trees and flaying them alive. In A.D. 61, her forces killed 70,000 Romans and temporarily retook Londinium before falling in defeat to the Roman army. The queen (whose name means victorious) became a heroic figure of Victorian England. This statue by Thomas Thornycroft was erected in 1902. *Bridge St. & Victoria Embankment.*

2 ★★ **kids Cabinet War Rooms.** Winston Churchill directed World War II from this underground shelter as German bombs rained down on London. The basements of the Civil Service buildings along King Charles Street were converted in 1938 and designed to hold over 500 people in an area of roughly 1.2 hectares (3 acres). A hospital,

William Churchill's desk inside the Cabinet War Rooms.

a cafeteria, sleeping quarters, and even a shooting range were established in the low, cramped rooms. After the war, the area was locked and left untouched until Churchill's quarters were turned into a museum in 1981; all the items you see are the genuine articles. *Clive Steps, King Charles St.* ☎ *0207/ 930-6961. http://cwr.iwm.org.uk.*

3 ★★ **kids Horse Guards Parade.** London's largest open space dates back to 1745 and offers excellent views of Whitehall's architecture. It's best known as the site for the annual Trooping of the Color ceremony to celebrate the queen's birthday. Every day at 11am (10am on Sun) there's a much mellower (and less crowded) Changing of the Guard than you'll find at Buckingham Palace (p 22, bullet **3**). *Horseguards Rd.*

4 ★★ **The Mall.** This thoroughfare—running west from Buckingham Palace (see p 45, bullet **1**) to Trafalgar Square (see p 22, bullet **6**)—was created in 1660 as an annex to St. James's Park for the gallants to play the popular game of *paille mall* (a precursor to croquet). In the early 18th century it was a fashionable promenade for the *beau monde,* and in 1903 it was redesigned as a processional route for royal occasions. When foreign heads of state visit the queen, the Mall is decked out in the Union Jack and the flags of the visitor's country. *Between Buckingham Palace and Admiralty Arch.*

5 ★ **Admiralty Arch.** Built in 1910, this quintuple-arched building looks west to the grand statue of Queen Victoria in front of Buckingham Palace. The central gates are for ceremonial use, opening only to let a royal procession pass. Note the adorable little ships sitting atop some of the nearby street lamps in a nod to the Old Admiralty Offices for which the arch was named.

6 ★★★ **Banqueting House.** All that remains of Whitehall Palace is this hall, completed in 1622 by Inigo Jones. The city's first Renaissance-style construction is best known for its glorious Rubens-painted ceiling—commissioned by Charles I (1600–49), who used the building to greet foreign envoys and as a venue for parties. The allegorical ceiling, equating the Stuart kings with the gods, may have gone to Charles's head—his belief in the divine right of kings led directly to the removal of that head when he was executed for treason in 1649 on a scaffold just outside the hall. *Whitehall.* ☎ *0207/839-3787. www.hrp.org.uk. Adults £4, kids & seniors £3. Mon–Sat 10am–5pm.*

A sentry and his mount at the Whitehall entrance to Horse Guards Parade.

7 **Horse Guards, Whitehall Entrance.** Just across from the Banqueting House is another entrance to Horse Guards Parade guarded by two mounted soldiers in ceremonial garb, who appear to do nothing but provide good photo ops for visitors. Go through the gates and have a look through the arched tunnel, framing a beautiful view of St. James's Park.

8 ★ **10 Downing Street.** The home address of Britain's prime minister since 1732 is set in a quiet cul-de-sac. The street was open to the public until 1990, when it was blocked off by iron gates for security reasons. There's not much to see now except a lot of security guards giving you the evil eye, though there is a *frisson* of excitement to be had while standing near so much power.

The Banqueting House, the last surviving remnant of Whitehall Palace.

Of the many fine pubs that line Whitehall, my favorite is the **9** **Silver Cross,** which, despite its faux ye olde England decor, is genuinely old (it was granted a brothel license in 1674). It offers good fish-and-chips, lots of seating, and its own ghost—a young girl in Tudor dress. *33 Whitehall.* ☎ *0207/930-8350. $* ●

Shopping Best Bets

Best **Time to Shop**
During the August and January citywide, month-long sales

Best **Shot at Last Season's Designer Threads**
★★★ **Pandora**, *16–22 Cheval Place* (p 79)

Best **Fashion Jewelry**
★★ **Butler & Wilson**, *189 Fulham Rd. (p 82)*

Best **Write Stuff**
★★★ **Smythson of Bond Street**, *40 New Bond St. (p 77)*

Best **Sugar Rush**
★★ **The Chocolate Society**, *36 Elizabeth St. (p 80)*

Best **Children's Toy Store**
★★★ **Daisy and Tom**, *181–183 King's Rd. (p 83)*

Best **Place to Score Stuff from Other People's Attics**
★★ **Antiquarius**, *131–141 King's Rd. (p 76)*

Chelsea's Antiquarius is home to a wide variety of antiques dealers.

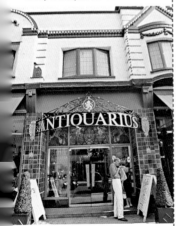

Best **Housewares**
★★ **India Jane**, *140 Sloane St. (p 81)*

Best **Foot Forward**
★★ **The Natural Shoe Store**, *21 Neal St. (p 78)*

Best **Historic Bookstore**
★★★ **Hatchards**, *187 Piccadilly (p 77)*

Best **Hot-Date Lingerie**
★★ **Agent Provocateur**, *6 Broadwick St. (p 82)*

Best **Kick-Back Knickers**
★ **Marks & Spencer**, *458 Oxford St. (p 82)*

Best **Gourmet Foods**
★★ **Fortnum & Mason**, *181 Piccadilly (p 80)*

Best **Place for Francophiles**
★★★ **Summerhill & Bishop**, *100 Portland St. (p 81)*

Best **Everything**
★★★ **Selfridges**, *400 Oxford St. (p 81)*

Best **Cosmetics**
★★ **Pout**, *32 Shelton St. (p 77)*

Best **Museum Shop**
★★★ **Victoria and Albert Museum**, *Cromwell Rd. (p 83)*

Best **Parfumerie**
★★ **Penhaligon's**, *16 Burlington Arcade (p 77)*

Best **Vintage Costume Jewelry**
★★★ **Steinberg & Tolkien**, *193 King's Rd. (p 78)*

Best **Wool Sweaters**
★★★ **Ireland in London**, *5 Montpelier St. (p 84)*

Best **Pinic Supplies**
★★ **Villandry**, *170 Great Portland St. (p 80)*

London Shopping

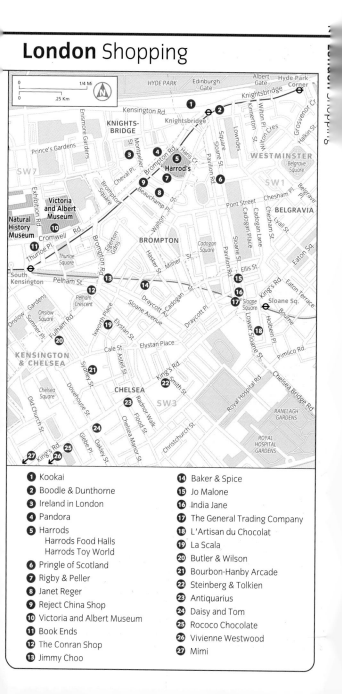

1. Kookai
2. Boodle & Dunthorne
3. Ireland in London
4. Pandora
5. Harrods
   Harrods Food Halls
   Harrods Toy World
6. Pringle of Scotland
7. Rigby & Peller
8. Janet Reger
9. Reject China Shop
10. Victoria and Albert Museum
11. Book Ends
12. The Conran Shop
13. Jimmy Choo
14. Baker & Spice
15. Jo Malone
16. India Jane
17. The General Trading Company
18. L'Artisan du Chocolat
19. La Scala
20. Butler & Wilson
21. Bourbon-Hanby Arcade
22. Steinberg & Tolkien
23. Antiquarius
24. Daisy and Tom
25. Rococo Chocolate
26. Vivienne Westwood
27. Mimi

Central London Shopping

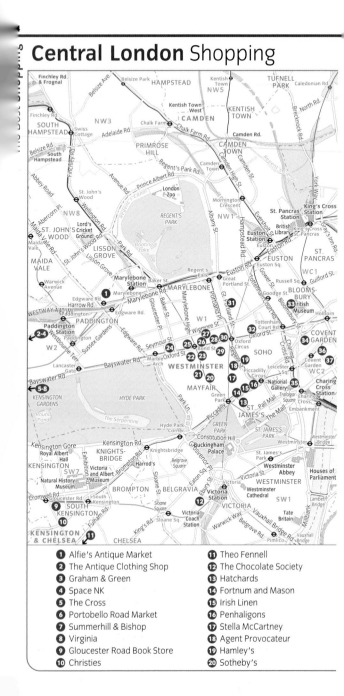

1. Alfie's Antique Market
2. The Antique Clothing Shop
3. Graham & Green
4. Space NK
5. The Cross
6. Portobello Road Market
7. Summerhill & Bishop
8. Virginia
9. Gloucester Road Book Store
10. Christies
11. Theo Fennell
12. The Chocolate Society
13. Hatchards
14. Fortnum and Mason
15. Irish Linen
16. Penhaligons
17. Stella McCartney
18. Agent Provocateur
19. Hamley's
20. Sotheby's

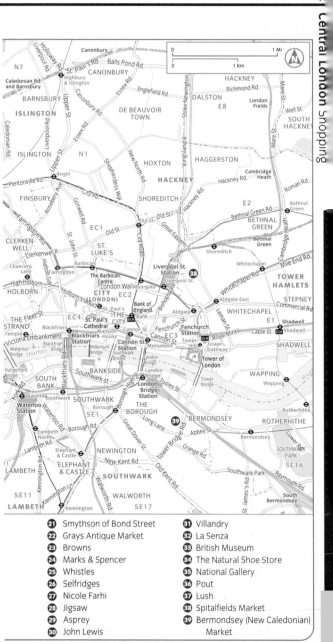

21	Smythson of Bond Street	**31**	Villandry
22	Grays Antique Market	**32**	La Senza
23	Browns	**33**	British Museum
24	Marks & Spencer	**34**	The Natural Shoe Store
25	Whistles	**35**	National Gallery
26	Selfridges	**36**	Pout
27	Nicole Farhi	**37**	Lush
28	Jigsaw	**38**	Spitalfields Market
29	Asprey	**39**	Bermondsey (New Caledonian)
30	John Lewis		Market

Shopping A to Z

Antiques and Art Auctions

★★ Alfie's Antique Market

MARYLEBONE   The city's largest collection of dealers—four floors of secondhand knickknacks, plus old fabrics and 1950s dresses. *13–25 Church St.* ☎ *0207/723-6066. www. alfiesantiques.com. Some dealers take credit cards. Tube: Marylebone or Edgware Rd. Map p 74.*

★★ Antiquarius CHELSEA   Some

120 stalls sell a fun assortment of both high-end and more affordable silver, antique jewelry, clocks, luggage, and art. *131–141 King's Rd.* ☎ *0207/351-5353. Some dealers take credit cards. Tube: Sloane Sq. Map p 73.*

★★ Bourbon-Hanby Arcade

CHELSEA   This rather grand collection of antiques stalls features upscale estate goods, jewelry, and fine art. *151 Sydney St.* ☎ *0207/ 352-2106. www.bourbonhanby.co.uk. Some dealers take credit cards. Tube: Sloane Sq. Map p 73.*

★★ Christie's SOUTH KENSINGTON

Don't be scared off by the cost of the serious treasures—this venerable auction house usually has something for all budgets. *85 Old Brompton Rd.* ☎ *0207/930-6074. www.christies.com. AE, MC, V. Tube: South Kensington. Map p 74.*

★★★ Grays Antique Market

MAYFAIR   Stalls here sell everything from Art Deco paperweights to antique jewelry to vintage Edwardian toys. *58 Davies St.* ☎ *0207/629-7034. www.graysantiques.com. Some dealers take credit cards. Tube: Bond St., Marble Arch. Map p 74.*

★★ Sotheby's MAYFAIR   The

stock here hinges on who's cleaning out their closets or moving house. Depending on the auction, you could spend £20 or £2 million. *34–35 New Bond St.* ☎ *0207/293-5000. www. sothebys.com. AE, MC, V. Tube: Bond St. Map p 74.*

Beauty Products

★★ Jo Malone CHELSEA

Although she now sells outside the U.K., Jo Malone's flagship shop is worth a visit for its heavenly perfumes and candles, or to pick up a gift or two. *150 Sloane St.* ☎ *0207/ 730-2100. www.jomalone.co.uk. AE, MC, V. Tube: Sloane Sq. Map p 73.*

★★ Lush COVENT GARDEN   This

chain offers unusual handmade bath and beauty goods, including bath

For unusual handmade bath and beauty products, you can't beat Lush.

Penhaligon's perfumes and toiletries meet even royal standards.

bombs and moisturizing soaps made from natural ingredients. *Unit 11, The Piazza, Covent Garden.* ☎ *0207/240-4570. www.lush.co.uk. AE, MC, V. Tube: Covent Garden. Map p 74.*

★ **Penhaligon's** MAYFAIR   Old but not stodgy, this royal favorite offers good value and great perfumed gifts; the bath oil and scented candle duo will sweeten up anyone's day. *16 Burlington Arcade.* ☎ *0207/629-1416. www.penhaligons. co.uk. AE, DC, MC, V. Tube: Green Park. Map p 74.*

★★★ **Pout** COVENT GARDEN   This shop is a make-up junkie's favorite fix: It's got everything you need—or crave. Their own very chic product line is a favorite of celebs. *32 Shelton St.* ☎ *0207/379-0379. www.pout.co. uk. AE, MC, V. Tube: Covent Garden. Map p 74.*

★★ **Space NK** NOTTING HILL This popular English chain sells many boutique-style lines of make-up, creams, fragrances, and decadently scented candles. *127–131 West-bourne Grove.* ☎ *0207/727-8063.*

www.spacenk.co.uk. AE, MC, V. Tube: Notting Hill Gate. Map p 74.

Books and Stationery
★★★ **Gloucester Road Book Store** KENSINGTON   Good prices on secondhand books that have been carefully culled by the knowledgeable staff. Check out the fabulous coffee mugs imprinted with old Penguin paperback covers. *123 Gloucester Rd.* ☎ *0207/370-3503. MC, V. Tube: Gloucester Rd. Map p 74.*

★★★ **Hatchards** PICCADILLY This home for discerning biblio-philes has been in business since 1797. It's tops for books on royalty. *187 Piccadilly.* ☎ *0207/439-9921. www.hatchards.co.uk. AE, DC, MC, V. Tube: Green Park. Map p 74.*

★★★ **Smythson of Bond Street** MAYFAIR   This expensive and exclusive stationer caters to generations of posh Londoners, who would feel naked without a Smythson appointment diary. *40 New Bond St.* ☎ *0207/629-8558. www.smythson.com. AE, DC, MC, V. Tube: Bond St. Map p 74.*

Clothing and Shoes

★★ The Antique Clothing Shop

NOTTING HILL   Lots of great old glad rags, plus rarer work get-ups from your great-grandmother's day. *282 Portobello Rd.* ☎ *0208/964-4830. AE. Tube: Ladbroke Grove. Map p 74.*

★★ Browns

MAYFAIR   The best place in town for up-to-the-minute fashions, including a discriminating collection of hip designers. Keep your eyes peeled for sales. *23–27 S. Moulton St.* ☎ *0207/514-0000. www.brownsfashions.com. AE, MC, V. Tube: Bond St. Map p 74.*

★★★ The Cross

HOLLAND PARK   Fashionistas in the know flock here for Missoni, Johnny Loves Rosie, Alice Lee, and other designers, plus some housewares and surprisingly witty children's gifts. *141 Portland Rd.* ☎ *0207/727-6760. AE, MC, V. Tube: Holland Park. Map p 74.*

★ Jigsaw

MAYFAIR   Quality clothes, quiet colors, and reasonable prices are what you'll find at this popular chain. The sweaters and trousers are particularly pleasing, if unadventurous. *126–127 New Bond St.* ☎ *0207/491-4484. www.jigsaw-online.com. AE, MC, V. Tube: Bond St. Map p 74.*

★★★ Jimmy Choo

SOUTH KENSINGTON   This London designer-turned-global brand pops up on the well-manicured feet of Oscar contenders and well-kept mistresses. You'll pay dearly for a pair. *169 Draycott Ave.* ☎ *0207/584-6111. www.jimmychoo.com. AE, MC, V. Tube: S. Kensington. Map p 73.*

★ Kookai

KNIGHTSBRIDGE   This sexy French chain store offers good value with its moderate-range, smart-casual clothes. Sizes run small. *5/7 Brompton Rd.* ☎ *0207/581-9633. www.kookai.co.uk. AE, DC, MC, V. Tube: Knightsbridge. Map p 73.*

★★ La Scala

CHELSEA   It's hit or miss inside this small shop, which offers deep discounts on second-hand designer clothes, courtesy of the seasonal closet-cleanings of Chelsea's upper crust. *39 Elystan St.* ☎ *0207/589-2784. AE, DC, MC, V. Tube: S. Kensington or Sloane Sq. Map p 73.*

★★ Mimi

CHELSEA   This little boutique carries clothes and accessories from trendsetters Anya Hindmarch, Juicy Couture, Cacherel, Matthew Williamson, and others. *309 King's Rd.* ☎ *0207/349-9699. AE, DC, MC, V. Tube: Sloane Sq., then bus no. 11. Map p 73.*

★★ The Natural Shoe Store

COVENT GARDEN   Come here for the best of Birkenstock, Ecco, Arche, and other comfortable hippie styles now totally in vogue. *21 Neal St.* ☎ *0207/836-5254. www.thenaturalshoestore.com. AE, DC, MC, V. Tube: Covent Garden. Map p 74.*

★★ Nicole Farhi

MAYFAIR   Nicole Farhi's masterful designs are the best in smart casual attire. Her comfy shirts are well made and look great with her tailored jackets. *158 New Bond St.* ☎ *0207/499-8368. www.nicolefarhi.com. AE, DC, MC, V. Tube: Green Park. Map p 74.*

For London's best business casual attire, head to Nicole Farhi.

It's overpriced, but Harrods is a London shopping institution.

★★★ Pandora KNIGHTSBRIDGE

A big, well-organized shop features lots of designer names, shoes, and accessories left on consignment by frightfully rich Knightsbridge clotheshorses. *16–22 Cheval Place.* ☎ *0207/589-5289. AE, MC, V. Tube: Knightsbridge. Map p 73.*

★★★ Steinberg & Tolkien

CHELSEA   Film costume designers come here for inspiration. Expect to find vintage clothing going back to the Victorian era, with lots of mod Carnaby Street '60s gear, plus accessories. *193 King's Rd.* ☎ *0207/376-3660. AE, MC, V. Tube: Sloane Sq. Map p 73.*

★★ Stella McCartney MAYFAIR

Stella McCartney has won more awards than most designers do in a lifetime, and her latest collection appeals to the young and beautiful (it helps to be rich, too). *30 Bruton St.* ☎ *0207/518-3100. www. stellamccartney.co.uk. AE, DC, MC, V. Tube: Green Park. Map p 74.*

★★ Virginia HOLLAND PARK   This

store, best for very thin rich women and historians of fashion, is outrageous in terms of price and the rarity of its vintage wares. Check out the beaded flapper dresses. *98 Portland Rd.* ☎ *0207/727-9908. AE, DC, MC, V. Tube: Holland Park. Map p 74.*

★★ Vivienne Westwood

CHELSEA   The undisputed English Queen of Fashion—her stuff's been exhibited at the V&A—caters to the young, stylish, and rich. This branch is the coolest of her London boutiques. *430 King's Rd.* ☎ *0207/439-1109. www.viviennewestwood. com. AE, DC, MC, V. Tube: Sloane Sq., then bus no. 11. Map p 73.*

★★ Whistles MARYLEBONE

Upmarket collections from trendy designers (Betty Jackson, for one) are the mainstay of this pricey shop, which also sells its own designs, including well-made separates and fancy dresses. *12 St. Christophers Place.* ☎ *0207/487-4484. AE, DC, MC, V. Tube: Marble Arch. Map p 74.*

Department Stores

★ Harrods KNIGHTSBRIDGE

From its food halls to its home entertainment centers, Harrods is a London institution—as well as an overhyped and overpriced bore. *87–135 Brompton Rd.* ☎ *0207/730-1234. www.harrods.com. AE, DC, MC, V. Tube: Knightsbridge. Map p 73.*

★★★ John Lewis MARYLEBONE

This is *the* place to find homey necessities such as sewing notions, fabrics, and kitchenware. Londoners can't live without it. *278–306 Oxford St.* ☎ *0207/629-7711. www.johnlewis. co.uk. AE, DC, MC, V. Tube: Oxford Circus. Map p 74.*

★★★ **Selfridges** MARYLEBONE Thanks to a major refurbishment, this grand old department store is the best in town. The food halls are great, as are the fashions; it even offers tattooing and piercing. *400 Oxford St.* ☎ *0870/837-7377. www.selfridges.com. AE, DC, MC, V. Tube: Marble Arch. Map p 74.*

Food and Chocolates
★★★ **Baker & Spice** CHELSEA This store bakes its high-priced delectables right on the premises; it's Londoners' guilty secret. *47 Denyer St.* ☎ *0207/589-4734. www.bakerandspice.com. MC, V. Tube: S. Kensington. Map p 73.*

★★★ **The Chocolate Society** PIMLICO With its amazing variations on a theme of cocoa beans, this shop offers truly killer chocolate for grown-up tastes. *36 Elizabeth St.* ☎ *0207/259-9222. www.chocolate. co.uk. MC, V. Tube: Victoria or Sloane Sq. Map p 74.*

★★ **Fortnum & Mason** MAYFAIR The city's ultimate grocer features goodies fit for the queen—or friends back home—plus gourmet picnic fare and specialty teas. *181 Piccadilly.* ☎ *0207/734-8040. www.fortnumandmason.co.uk.*

The ultimate London grocer, Fortnum & Mason can furnish a feast fit for a queen.

AE, DC, MC, V. Tube: Green Park. Map p 74.

★ **Harrods Food Halls** KNIGHTS-BRIDGE Harrods sells loads of edible gifts branded with its famous name; be sure to ogle the remarkable ceilings in the produce and meat sections. *87–135 Brompton Rd.* ☎ *0207/730-1234. www.harrods. com. AE, DC, MC, V. Tube: Knightsbridge. Map p 73.*

★★ **L'Artisan du Chocolat** CHELSEA This award-winning shop makes quirky and delicious flavored chocolates and truffles for the connoisseur. Try the lavender chocolate—close your eyes, and you'll be in Provence. *89 Lower Sloane St.* ☎ *0207/824-8365. www.artisanduchocolat.com. MC, V. Tube: Sloane Sq. Map p 73.*

★★ **Rococo Chocolate** CHELSEA Chocoholics should head to this fine store, which stocks wittily shaped, high-cocoa-content confections and unique flavors (Earl Grey, rose, and more). *321 King's Rd.* ☎ *0207/352-5857. www.rococochocolates.com. MC, V. Tube: Sloan Sq., then bus no. 11. Map p 73.*

★★ **Villandry** MARYLEBONE Hearty foodstuffs are sold in a pleasing and unpretentious setting at this store, which is a great place to buy picnic supplies. *170 Great Portland St.* ☎ *0207/631-3131. www.villandry.com. AE, DC, MC, V. Tube: Great Portland St. Map p 74.*

Home Decor
★★ **The Conran Shop** SOUTH KENSINGTON Your best bets among the large and varied selection of high-priced merchandise here are the fabrics, the kitchenware, and the bath items. *Michelin House, 81 Fulham Rd.* ☎ *0207/589-7401. www.conran.com. AE, MC, V. Tube: S. Kensington. Map p 73.*

Asprey, the royal jeweler, offers a world-class collection of gems.

★★★ The General Trading Company
CHELSEA   Started in the 1920s, this shop sells household knickknacks, as well as furniture from every corner of the Empire. *2 Symons St.* ☎ *0207/730-0411. www.general-trading.co.uk. AE, MC, V. Tube: Sloane Sq. Map p 73.*

★ Graham & Green
NOTTING HILL   Lighting, stationery, and attractive home-decor whatnots fill Graham & Green's two shops, located across the street from one another. *4 and 10 Elgin Crescent.* ☎ *0207/727-4594. www.graham andgreen.co.uk. AE, MC, V. Tube: Notting Hill. Map p 74.*

★★ India Jane
CHELSEA   This wholesaler culls the best of India's most dignified home furnishings and sells them to the public. *140 Sloane St.* ☎ *0207/730-1070. AE, MC, V. Tube: Sloane Sq. Map p 73.*

★★★ Reject China Shop
KNIGHTSBRIDGE   Forget finding too many rejects here. This retailer sells complete sets (as well as single plates) of first-class Spode, Wedgwood, Doulton, and others. Free shipping for orders over £300. *183 Brompton Rd.* ☎ *0207/581-0739. www.tableware.uk.com. AE, DC, MC, V. Tube: Knightsbridge. Map p 73.*

★★★ Summerhill & Bishop
HOLLAND PARK   Shop here for a sumptuous collection of French housewares, from efficient, humble radiator dusters to the finest table settings and cookery. *100 Portland St.* ☎ *0207/221-4566. AE, MC, V. Tube: Holland Park. Map p 74.*

Jewelry

★★★ Asprey
MAYFAIR   This royal jeweler has dropped the "& Garrard" from its name, but you'll still need to bring your platinum card if you want to invest in Asprey's world-class collection of jewels, gems, and watches. *167 New Bond St.* ☎ *0207/493-6767. www.asprey.com. AE, DC, MC, V. Tube: Bond St. Map p 74.*

★ Boodle & Dunthorne
KNIGHTS-BRIDGE   One of England's oldest jewelers (open since 1798), B&D has

resident designers who keep its collection fresh and modern. *1 Sloane St.* ☎ *0207/235-0111. www.boodle anddunthorne.com. AE, DC, MC, V. Tube: Knightsbridge. Map p 73.*

★ **Butler & Wilson** SOUTH KENSINGTON   You won't have to remortgage your house to buy this store's beautiful costume and silver jewelry. It's *the* place in town for tiaras. *189 Fulham Rd.* ☎ *0207/352-8255. www.butlerandwilson.co.uk. AE, MC, V. Tube: S. Kensington. Map p 73.*

★★★ **Theo Fennell** SOUTH KENSINGTON   Visit one of London's most beloved jewelry designers for pieces that are sleek and modern, but with classic touches. *169 Fulham Rd.* ☎ *0207/591-5000. www. theofennell.com. AE, DC, MC, V. Tube: S. Kensington. Map p 74.*

Lingerie

★★ **Agent Provocateur** SOHO   Provocative, indeed! This store's sexy underclothes are works of art. If you've fallen off your diet, don't bother walking inside. *6 Broadwick St.* ☎ *0207/439-0229. www.agent provocateur.com. AE, DC, MC, V. Tube: Piccadilly. Map p 74.*

★★ **Janet Reger** KNIGHTSBRIDGE   This small shop sells even tinier merchandise: beautiful bras, panties, and baby-doll under-slips. *2 Beauchamp Place.* ☎ *0207/584-9360. www. janetreger.com. AE, MC, V. Tube: Knightsbridge. Map p 73.*

★★ **La Senza** FITZROVIA   Come here for classy, well-made lingerie; the bras are almost too beautiful to hide beneath clothing. *162 Oxford St.* ☎ *0207/580-3559. www.lasenza. com. AE, DC, MC, V. Tube: Oxford Circus. Map p 74.*

★ **Marks & Spencer** MARYLEBONE   This beloved, reliable outlet for comfy cotton underwear for men and women has kept up with the times, and offers a lot more than old-lady knickers. *458 Oxford St.* ☎ *0207/935-7954. www.marksand spencer.com. AE, DC, MC, V. Tube: Marble Arch. Map p 74.*

★ **Rigby & Peller** KNIGHTSBRIDGE   The corsetiere to the queen specializes in classy underwear, bathing suits (ask for "swimming costumes"), and finely engineered brassieres. *2 Hans Rd.* ☎ *0207/589-9293. www. rigbyandpeller.com. AE, DC, MC, V. Tube: Knightsbridge. Map p 73.*

Markets

★ **Bermondsey (New Caledonian) Market** BERMONDSEY   If you're up at 4am on a Friday, join the crush of dealers fighting over the estate goods and antiques sold here. *Corner of Bermondsey St. and Long Lane.* ☎ *0207/969-1500. Some dealers take credit cards. Tube: Bermondsey. Map p 74.*

★★★ **Portobello Road Market** NOTTING HILL   Saturday is the best day to join the throngs at Portobello's famous antiques market. Bring cash if you want the best deals. *Portobello Rd. (from Notting Hill end to Ladbroke Grove). Some dealers take major credit cards. Tube: Notting Hill. Map p 74.*

★★ **Spitalfield Market** SHOREDITCH   Head to Spitalfield's huge covered market on Sunday for organic produce, ethnic clothes, knickknacks, and handmade crafts. *Commercial St.* ☎ *0207/247-8556.*

Organic produce at Spitalfield Market.

A Harry Potter made of LEGOs is just one of Hamley's spectacular toys.

Most dealers take cash only. Tube: Liverpool St. Map p 74.

Museum Shops

★ kids British Museum

BLOOMSBURY   The B.M. sells inexpensive key chains, children's toys, fine reproductions, gorgeous scarves, and great T-shirts themed to its collections. *Great Russell St.* ☎ *0207/636-1555. www.thebritish museum.ac.uk. AE, DC, MC, V. Tube: Russell Sq. Map p 74.*

★★ National Gallery THE WEST

END   The city's best source for art-related books and stationery, this shop also sells excellent calendars, cool T-shirts, and lots of quirky, artsy gifts. *Trafalgar Sq.* ☎ *0207/ 747-2885. www.nationalgallery.org.uk. AE, DC, MC, V. Tube: Charing Cross. Map p 74.*

★★★ kids Victoria and Albert

Museum SOUTH KENSINGTON This must-stop shop sells everything from postcards to jewelry. Cool finds include plates with Sèvres designs and children's gifts. *Cromwell Rd.* ☎ *0207/942-2000. www.vam.ac.uk. AE, DC, MC, V. Tube: S. Kensington. Map p 73.*

Toys

★★ kids Book Ends SOUTH KENS-

INGTON   Your best bet for easy-to-carry-home gifts for kids. There's an excellent range of crafts, children's books on London, coloring books, and art supplies. *25–28 Thurloe Place.* ☎ *0207/589-2285. AE, MC, V. Tube: S. Kensington. Map p 73.*

★★★ kids Daisy and Tom

CHELSEA   This one-stop children's store offers a kaleidoscopic array of toys, books, and clothes in a kid-friendly setting that features puppet shows on weekends. *181–183 King's Rd.* ☎ *0207/352-5000. www.daisyandtom.com. AE, DC, MC, V. Tube: Sloane Sq. Map p 73.*

★ kids Hamley's PICCADILLY

London's answer to F.A.O. Schwarz sports seven floors of fun and games. There's a huge selection of more than 35,000 toys from all over the world. *189–196 Regent St.* ☎ *0870/333-2455. www.hamleys. com. AE, DC, MC, V. Tube: Piccadilly Circus. Map p 74.*

The National Gallery sells prints of its masterpieces, including Jan Van Eyck's Arnolfini Marriage.

★ kids Harrods Toy World

KNIGHTSBRIDGE   Something for all ages, plus kiddie-size cars and life-size stuffed animals. Be prepared for a bad case of the "gimmes" from your kids. *4th Floor, 87–135 Brompton Rd.* ☎ *0207/730-1234. www.harrods.com. AE, DC, MC, V. Tube: Knightsbridge. Map p 73.*

Woolens and Linens
★★★ Ireland in London

KNIGHTSBRIDGE   This shop carries the best Irish woolens in London, including thick cable-knit fishermen sweaters and gorgeous mohair throws. It's also good for fine linens and crystal. *5 Montpelier St.* ☎ *0207/589-4455. www.irelandin london.com. AE, DC, MC, V. Tube: Sloane Sq. Map p 73.*

★★ Irish Linen

MAYFAIR   The shop carries a fine, rather expensive selection of bed sheets accented with lace (don't be put off by the stiffness), tablecloths, napkins, and nightgowns. *35–36 Burlington Arcade.* ☎ *0207/493-8949. AE, MC, V. Tube: Green Park. Map p 74.*

Selfridges is the best department store in London (see p 80).

★★ Pringle of Scotland

CHELSEA   Putting its rep for corn-ball golf cardigans behind it, this luxury retailer now sells an assortment of dressy casual-wear and woolens that are very much up to the minute. *141 Sloane St.* ☎ *0207/259-1660. www.pringle-of-scotland.co.uk. AE, DC, MC, V. Tube: Sloane Sq. Map p 73.* ●

VAT (Value Added Tax)

The U.K. levies a crushing 17.5% Value Added Tax (VAT) on all goods. (VAT is included in the price tag, unless it clearly states "plus VAT.") If you have your purchases sent home, you can avoid the VAT, but you must pay shipping and duty fees. Most shops will help you get a partial refund of the VAT (usually 13%–15%) if you spend a minimum of £50. Ask for a VAT form when you pay for an item and have it filled out *in the shop*—forms must be validated by the seller for you to claim your refund! When you get to the airport, present your form, passport, and purchases—do not pack them in your checked luggage—to the Customs agency for certification. Once your papers have been stamped, you can get a cash refund from one of the agencies at the airport (minus a service charge), or you can mail in the forms to get a cash or credit card refund. The process is a hassle and only worth going through for high-ticket items. For more information, go to www.hmce.gov.uk or www.visitbritain.com.

Hyde Park

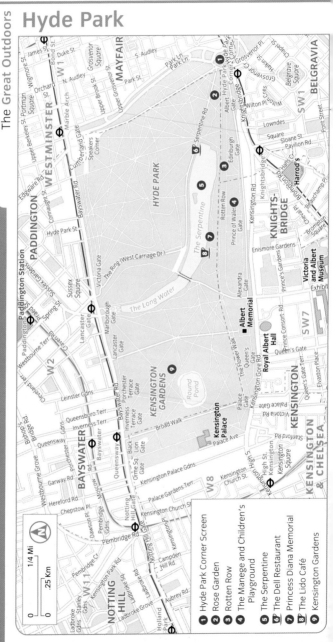

1. Hyde Park Corner Screen
2. Rose Garden
3. Rotten Row
4. The Manege and Children's Playground
5. The Serpentine
6. The Dell Restaurant
7. Princess Diana Memorial
8. The Lido Café
9. Kensington Gardens

Since 1536, when Henry VIII appropriated the land from the monks of Westminster Abbey for hunting, 142-hectare (350-acre) Hyde Park has been the scene of duels, highway robbery, and sport. Today, this Royal Park, the site of London's Great Exhibition of 1851, is a beloved oasis of green in the midst of the city, the best place for horseback riding in London, and a wonderful place to watch Londoners at play. START: **Hyde Park Corner Tube Station**

1 ★★ Hyde Park Corner Screen. Erected in 1828, this imposing park entrance (one of six park entryways) was designed by Decimus Burton, the noted architect responsible for much of Hyde Park's layout. The triple-arched screen is composed of Ionic columns, bronzed ironwork, and carved friezes inspired by the Elgin Marbles (p 31, bullet **3**). Unfortunately, it's being degraded by all the pollution at this busy traffic circle. ⏱ *10 min.*

2 ★★ kids Rose Garden. From the Rose Garden, a riot of color in the early summer, you can admire the back of Apsley House (p 21, bullet **2**) and Wellington Arch's elaborate statue, *Winged Victory* (erected to commemorate the Duke of Wellington's gallantry), in the east. The garden is filled with fountains and climbing rose trellises, both much loved by kids. Its central fountain is ringed with benches where

you can sit with a picnic lunch as hopeful (and picturesque) sparrows flutter around. ⏱ *20–30 min.*

3 ★★ kids Rotten Row. In the late 1680s, William III ordered 300 lamps to be hung from trees along this 2.4km (1.5-mile) riding path—whose name is an English corruption of its original appellation, *Route de Roi* ("King's Road")—in a vain attempt to stop the plague of highwaymen active in the park. Nowadays, it's the path where horses carrying riders through the park often decide it's time to canter, possibly sensing the echoes of the wild and dangerous carriage races that took place here over a century ago. If you want to give it a try, the best horses in the park are at the **Ross Nye Stables,** 8 Bathurst Mews (☎ 0207/262-3791). ⏱ *1 hr. On the southern boundary of the park. 1-hr. rides start at £40.*

Many Londoners retreat to Hyde Park for peace and quiet.

④ ★★★ kids The Manege and Children's Playground. At the Manege, a special riding arena for royal steeds, you may be lucky enough to see all the queen's men exercising all the queen's horses or practicing for a ceremonial event. The adjacent playground has all the equipment a kid might want, plus a nice view of the riding ring. *Off S. Carriage Dr.*

⑤ ★★★ kids The Serpentine. Queen Caroline had the Westbourne River dammed in 1730 to create the Serpentine Lake, upon which she moored two royal yachts. This lovely lake is now the premiere boating spot in London for the masses. Should you venture out on the water, your yacht will be a tad less splendid than the queen's—you can choose from among 110 paddle boats and rowboats at the Boat House. If you want to sit out an adventure on the high seas, you can entertain yourself watching the in-line skaters who love this stretch of the park. ⏱ *1 hr. Bluebird Boats Ltd., Serpentine Rd.* ☎ *0207/262-1330. Hourly rentals £6 adults, £2.50 kids, £15 family. Mar–Oct 10am–5pm.*

Hyde Park's Serpentine is London's best spot for boating.

was opened by the queen in July 2004. No less dogged by controversy than the woman who inspired it, the 700-ton, £6.5-million fountain has suffered from flooding, closures, and a slippery bottom. Children, who were meant to splash around happily in its cascading waters, are now restricted to toe-dipping by the omnipresent security guards. ⏱ *20 min. Near the Lido, south of the Serpentine.*

⑧ ★ kids The Lido Café offers blah food but is a good spot for a bathroom break, a cuppa, and good views. Sitting on the outdoor terrace, you may see people swimming in the adjacent Lido Pool, unfazed by the geese droppings. *South side of the Serpentine Terrace.* ☎ *0207/706-7098. $*

⑥ ★★ kids The Dell Restaurant has the best view of the Serpentine in the park, and serves hot meals, sandwiches, and drinks (wine included) that are a cut above the usual park cafeteria cuisine. You're welcome to picnic on the tables outside. *Eastern side of the Serpentine.* ☎ *0207/706-0464. $*

⑦ ★ kids Princess Diana Memorial. This contemporary granite fountain, across the Serpentine from the Boat House,

⑨ ★★★ kids Kensington Gardens. Originally a part of Hyde Park, the 111-hectare (275-acre) Kensington Gardens were partitioned into an exclusive preserve of

Kensington Garden's famous statue of Peter Pan, see (p 89).

royalty in the 18th century, and were opened to the public only in the early 1800s. Originally laid out in Dutch style (emphasizing water, avenues, and topiaries), the attractive gardens are especially popular with families.

Kensington Gardens Highlights

The bronze **9A** ★★ kids **Peter Pan Statue** was sculpted in 1912 by Sir George Frampton at the behest of author J. M. Barrie and is the most visited landmark in the park. A short walk north and you'll arrive at **9B** ★★★ kids **The Italian Gardens,** which echoed the rage for all things Italian when it was built in 1861. Generations of children have plied model boats at the **9C** ★★★ kids **Round Pond,** built in 1728. Today you'll also find adults trying out more sophisticated models. West of the pond is the **9D** **Broad Walk.** Nineteenth-century ladies and gentlemen promenaded along this tree-lined path past Kensington Palace, and flirted by the nearby bandstand. Peek through the front gates of Kensington Palace at the **9E** ★★★ kids **Sunken Gardens,** which were planted in 1909 and inspired by the Tudor gardens at Hampton Court Palace. End your tour at the exquisite **9F** ★★★ kids **Orangery Café,** where a very good tea is offered, and the atmosphere is airy and refined. ⏱ *2–3 hr. Go in the afternoon.* ☎ *0207/ 298-2100. www.royalparks.gov.uk. Tube: Kensington High St., Queensway, or Lancaster Gate.* $

Regent's Park

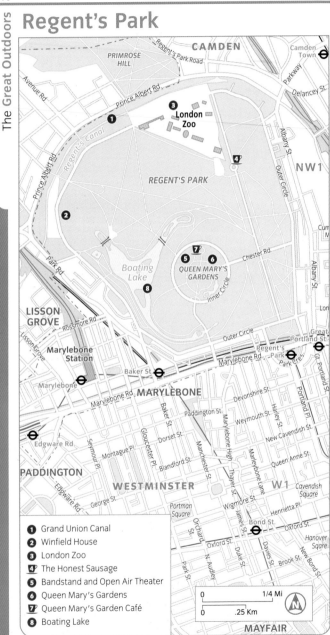

1 Grand Union Canal
2 Winfield House
3 London Zoo
4 The Honest Sausage
5 Bandstand and Open Air Theater
6 Queen Mary's Gardens
7 Queen Mary's Garden Café
8 Boating Lake

This 197-hectare (487-acre) gem started out as a hunting ground for Henry VIII, who liked to gallop here from Whitehall for the exercise. The park's ambitious design by John Nash (1752–1835) followed the romantic ideal of *rus in urbe* (country in the city), but what I love best about it is the carefully created sophistication of its many flower beds, its formal gardens with fountains, and the ornamental lake with its bridge and rowboats. It's more *urbe* than *rus* with its civilized decorative features and activities, and the leafy paths are lined with benches good for conversations, sunning, or people-watching. START: **Camden Town Station**

① ★★ kids Grand Union Canal. Londoners once traveled the city by boat when Regent's Park was in its infancy, and this is your chance to follow in their wake. The Grand Union Canal, opened in 1814, now covers 220km (137 miles) of waterways connecting the river Thames and the Chiltern Hills in Oxfordshire. Water buses now ply the scenic Regent's Canal section (opened in 1820) and will take you from Camden Lock's markets through the neighborhoods of colorful houseboats and grand Victorian houses on either side of the canal path in Little Venice—an area whose name is more wishful than accurate (there's just the one canal). Your final destination is the London Zoo inside Regent's Park. A combo ticket that covers boat fare and the London Zoo (£14) may not save you lots of money but is very convenient. ⏱ 50 min. Camden Lock. ☎ 0207/482-2660. www.londonwaterbus.com. One-way tickets £5.20 adults, £3.40 kids 3–15. Year-round, depending on the weather.

② Winfield House. As you sail, notice to your left the 4.6m (15-ft.) gates protecting a fine mansion beyond. Woolworth heiress Barbara Hutton built this Georgian mansion in 1936, adding extensive gardens and trees. A year after World War II, Hutton donated the antique-filled home to the American government for use as the official residence of the U.S. ambassador. Unfortunately, you have to be an invited guest to enter.

Boats line the Grand Union Canal in Regent's Park.

❸ ★★★ kids London Zoo.

When this former zoology center opened to the public in 1847, many of its captives, such as Jumbo the Elephant (later bought by P. T. Barnum and shipped off to the U.S.), were celebrities. Visitors who complain about the high price of admission might feel differently about this venerable institution if they knew that roughly one-sixth of its 650 species (about 5,000 animals reside here) are endangered—and that the zoo's world-renowned breeding program is the only thing preventing their extinction. I'm particularly fond of the reptile house (where Harry Potter learned the language of snakes), the gorillas, and the other simians. ⏱ *2 hr.; longer for families. Outer Circle, Regent's Park.* ☎ *0207/ 722-3333. www.londonzoo.co.uk. £13 adults, £11 seniors, £9.75 kids 3–15, £41 family. Daily 10am–4pm.*

If the smell of frying onions at ④P ★★ **The Honest Sausage** doesn't whet your appetite, nothing will. The menu features organic and relatively healthy lunch options. Best of all, there's a covered veranda to shelter you from sun and rain. *Broadwalk, Regent's Park.* ☎ *0207/ 224-3872. $*

❺ Bandstand and Open Air Theater.

From late May to early September, these two stages feature alfresco concerts and plays, most notably Shakespearean comedies staged by the English Shakespeare Company. See p 133.

❻ ★★★ kids Queen Mary's Gardens.

Laid out in the 1930s, these regal gardens lie at the heart of the park's Inner Circle and are a place of enchanting colors, fragrances, and watery vistas. The fabulous and carefully tended Rose

A lioness watches snow fall on the Regent's Park Zoo.

Gardens are especially beautiful in spring. ⏱ *30 min. Inner Circle.*

Food kiosks scattered around Regent's Park offer sandwiches and drinks. A less informal option is ⑦P ★★ **Queen Mary's Garden Café**, which sells a good variety of salads and sandwiches, as well as wine and beer, that you can enjoy on a lovely terrace. *Queen Mary's Garden, adjacent to Rose Garden.* ☎ *0207/935-5729. $*

❽ ★★ kids Boating Lake.

Operating on a schedule that changes with the weather, Park Boats rents paddle boats and rowboats you can take out on this picturesque lake. Though the concession is usually closed midweek and in winter, you may be able to go boating on any sunny warm day, whatever the season—be sure to call ahead. ⏱ *1 hr.* ☎ *0207/724-4069. Open weekends Mar–Nov 11am–6pm. Hourly rentals £6 adults, £4 kids, £18 family.* ●

The Best Dining

Dining **Best Bets**

Best **for Keeping Kids Happy**
★ Rainforest Café $$ 20–24 Shafts-bury Ave. (p 105)

Best **Vegetarian**
★★★ Mildred's $ 45 Lexington St. (p 103); or ★★ Food for Thought $ 31 Neal St. (p 101)

Best **Place for Beef**
★★★ Gaucho Grill $$ 19 Swallow St. (p 101)

Best **Pre-Theater Dining**
★★★ The Criterion Brasserie $$$ 224 Piccadilly (p 101)

Best **Neighborhood Italian**
★★★ Orsini's Cafe $ 8a Thurloe Place (p 104)

Best **Japanese**
★★★ Nobu $$$ 19 Old Park Lane (p 104)

Best **Luxe Afternoon Tea**
★★★ The Ritz Palm Court $$$ 150 Piccadilly (p 105)

Best **Deal on Afternoon Tea**
★★★ Basil Street Hotel $$ Basil St. (p 100); or ★★ Cadogan Hotel $ 75 Sloan St. (p 100)

Best **Cheap Eats**
★ Café in the Crypt $ St. Martin-in-the-Fields, Duncannon St. (p 101)

Best **American Noshes**
★ Ed's Easy Diner $ 362 King's Rd. (p 101)

Best **Classic Seafood**
★★★ Poisonnerie de l'Avenue $$$ 82 Sloane Ave. (p 104)

Best **Olde England Vibe**
★★ Rules $$ 35 Maiden Lane (p 105)

Best **View**
★★ Oxo Tower Brasserie $$ Oxo Tower Wharf, Bargehouse St.

The Ivy's the best dining spot in town for spotting celebrities.

(p 104); or ★★ The People's Palace $$$ Royal Festival Hall (p 104)

Best **Star Gazing**
★★ The Ivy $$ 1 West St. (p 102)

Best **Extravagant**
★★★ Gordon Ramsay $$$$$ 68 Royal Hospital Rd. (p 102)

Best **Middle Eastern**
★★★ Fahkreldine $$ 85 Piccadilly (p 101)

Best **Chinese**
★★ The Good Earth $$ 233 Brompton Rd. (p 102)

Best **French**
★★★ Le Gavroche $$$$$ 43 Upper Brook St. (p 103)

Best **Morroccan**
★★★ Momo $$ 25 Heddon St. (p 103)

Best **Indian**
★★ Tamarind $$$ 20 Queen St. (p 106)

Most **Romantic**
★★★ Lindsay House $$$$ 21 Romilly St. (p 103)

South Bank Dining

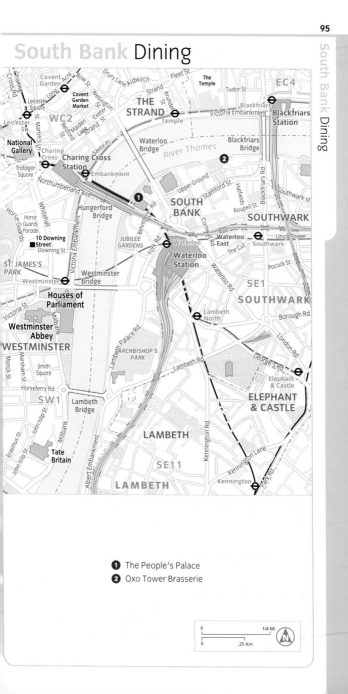

❶ The People's Palace

❷ Oxo Tower Brasserie

0   1/4 Mi

0   .25 Km

Knightsbridge Dining

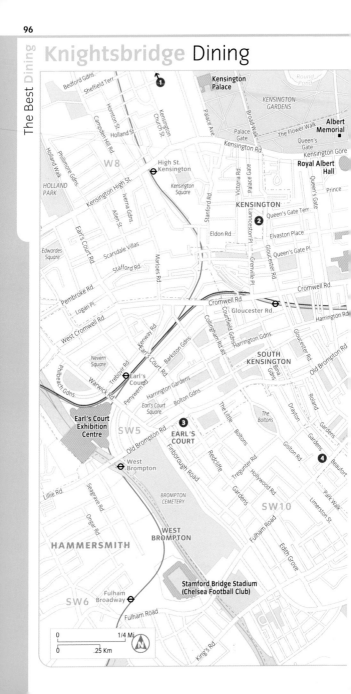

1. Kensington Place
2. Jakob's
3. Balans
4. Vingt Quatre
5. Ed's Easy Diner
6. My Old Dutch Pancake House
7. Gordon Ramsay
8. Poisonnerie de l'avenue
9. Itsu
10. Bibendum
11. Le Brasserie
12. The Collection
13. Café Creperie of Hampstead
14. Orsini's Cafe
15. Brasserie St. Quentin
16. Racine
17. The Good Earth
18. Patisserie Valerie
19. San Lorenzo
20. Cadogan Hotel
21. Basil Street Hotel
22. Pizza on the Park

West End Dining

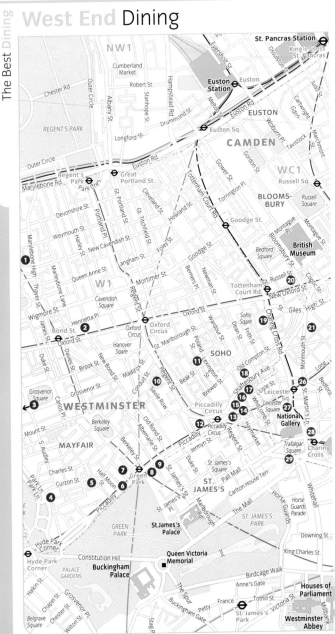

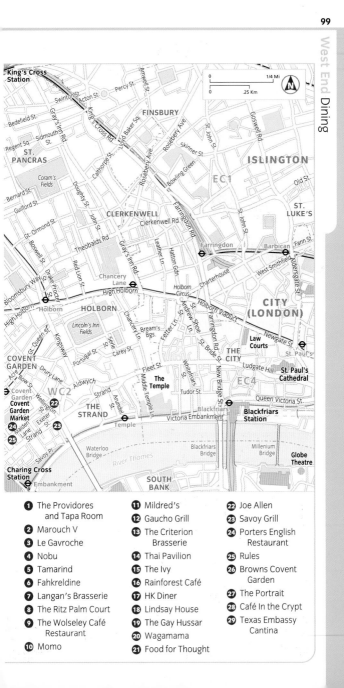

1 The Providores and Tapa Room
2 Marouch V
3 Le Gavroche
4 Nobu
5 Tamarind
6 Fahkreldine
7 Langan's Brasserie
8 The Ritz Palm Court
9 The Wolseley Café Restaurant
10 Momo
11 Mildred's
12 Gaucho Grill
13 The Criterion Brasserie
14 Thai Pavilion
15 The Ivy
16 Rainforest Café
17 HK Diner
18 Lindsay House
19 The Gay Hussar
20 Wagamama
21 Food for Thought
22 Joe Allen
23 Savoy Grill
24 Porters English Restaurant
25 Rules
26 Browns Covent Garden
27 The Portrait
28 Café In the Crypt
29 Texas Embassy Cantina

Restaurants A to Z

Bibendum and its oyster bar serve up some of London's freshest seafood.

★★ **kids** **Balans** EARLS COURT *MODERN BRITISH* The reasonably priced and varied menu make this an old reliable for breakfast, lunch, and dinner. *249 Old Brompton Rd. ☎ 0207/244-8838. Entrees £8–£15. AE, DC, MC, V. Breakfast, lunch & dinner daily. Tube: Earl's Court. Map p 96.*

★★★ **kids** **Basil Street Hotel** KNIGHTSBRIDGE *AFTERNOON TEA* This *veddy* English hotel serves a grand afternoon tea in a comfy and attractive parlor for a reasonable price. *Basil St. ☎ 0207/581-3311. Daily afternoon tea per person £17. AE, DC, MC, V. Tube: Knightsbridge. Map p 96.*

★★★ **Bibendum** SOUTH KENSINGTON *FRENCH/MEDITERRANEAN* Fresh fish served in light sauces, a great chef, and a location in the stylish Art Nouveau Michelin Building make this restaurant a winner. *81 Fulham Rd. ☎ 0207/581-5817. Entrees £20–£30. AE, DC, MC, V. Lunch & dinner daily. Tube: S. Kensington. Map p 96.*

★★★ **Brasserie St. Quentin** KNIGHTSBRIDGE *CLASSIC FRENCH* Chef Nana Akufo has made this classy Paris-style brasserie shine with his simple but delicious cuisine. *243 Brompton Rd. ☎ 0207/589-8005. Entrees £11–£20. AE, DC, MC, V. Lunch & dinner daily. Tube: Knightsbridge. Map p 96.*

★★ **kids** **Browns Covent Garden** COVENT GARDEN *MODERN BRITISH* The efficient service at this 300-seater, which sports a big menu and potted palm decor, makes it a good bet for pre-theater eats. *82–84 St. Martin's Lane.*

0207/497-5050. *Entrees £15–£20. AE, DC, MC, V. Lunch & dinner daily. Tube: Leicester Sq. Map p 98.*

★★ **Cadogan Hotel** CHELSEA
TEATIME The afternoon cream tea in the hotel's Drawing Room offers excellent value. You'll love the crustless sandwiches and scones, followed by tempting little pastries. *75 Sloane St.* 0207/235-7141. *Daily full afternoon tea £13 per person. AE, DC, MC, V. Tube: Sloane Sq. Map p 96.*

★ kids **Café Creperie of Hampstead** SOUTH KENSINGTON FRENCH
Treat yourself to one of this authentic French creperie's many savory galettes and sweet crepes. *2 Exhibition Rd.* 0207/589-8947. *Entrees £4–£8. MC, V. Lunch & dinner daily. Tube: S. Kensington. Map p 96.*

★ kids **Café In the Crypt** SOHO
BRITISH DINER This award-winning cafeteria offers cheap and hearty meals, as well as a jolly good tea. *St. Martin-in-the-Fields, enter on Duncannon St.* 0207/766-1129. *Entrees £3–£10. MC, V. Lunch & dinner daily. Tube: Charing Cross. Map p 98.*

★★ kids **The Collection**
CHELSEA INTERNATIONAL This oh-so-posh spot serves up an eclectic menu based on fresh and organic ingredients, and a kid-friendly weekend brunch. The sea bass is top-notch. *264 Brompton Rd.* 0207/225-1212. *Entrees £12–£20. AE, MC, V. Dinner daily. Tube: S. Kensington. Map p 96.*

★★★ **The Criterion Brasserie**
PICCADILLY FRENCH Top-rated chef Marco Pierre White serves high-quality brasserie cuisine in an opulent dining room that dates back to the Belle Epoque. *224 Piccadilly.* 0207/930-0488. *Entrees £15–£25. AE, DC, MC, V. Lunch & dinner Mon–Sat. Tube: Piccadilly. Map p 98.*

★ kids **Ed's Easy Diner** CHELSEA
AMERICAN This '50s-style diner is the only place in London that comes close to making good old American milkshakes, burgers, and fries. *362 King's Rd.* 0207/352-1956. *Entrees £7–£15. AE, DC, MC, V. Lunch & dinner daily. Tube: Sloane Sq. Map p 96.*

★★★ kids **Fahkreldine** MAYFAIR
LEBANESE London's best Lebanese restaurant, thanks to its traditional menu, solid service, and fine views of Green Park. *85 Piccadilly.* 0207/493-3424. *Entrees £12–£20. AE, MC, V. Lunch & dinner daily; Sun brunch. Tube: Green Park. Map p 98.*

★★ kids **Food for Thought**
COVENT GARDEN VEGETARIAN
It's a hole-in-the-wall with just a few tables, but the food is fresh, vegetarian, imaginative, and very healthy. *31 Neal St.* 0207/836-0239. *Entrees £5–£8. No credit cards. Breakfast, lunch & dinner Mon–Sat; lunch Sun. Tube: Covent Garden. Map p 98.*

★★★ kids **Gaucho Grill** WEST END ARGENTINEAN The best Argentinean dining in Europe, with an emphasis on grilled beef. There's also a small selection of South American wines. *19 Swallow St.* 0207/734-4040. *Entrees £10–£30. AE, DC, MC, V. Lunch & dinner daily. Tube: Piccadilly. Map p 98.*

There's no better place for a milkshake than Ed's Easy Diner.

★★ **The Gay Hussar** SOHO
HUNGARIAN Since 1953, this tiny dining room has served tasty goulashes, potato pancakes, blini, and other comfort foods to locals and tourists. *2 Greek St.* ☎ *0207/437-0973. Entrees £10–£20. MC, V. Lunch & dinner daily. Tube: Tottenham Court. Map p 98.*

★★ **kids The Good Earth**
KNIGHTSBRIDGE *CHINESE* More elegant than your usual Chinese restaurant, with prices to match, this Knightsbridge favorite does a great Beijing duck. It's good for vegetarians, too. *233 Brompton Rd.* ☎ *0207/584-3658. Entrees £12–£20. AE, MC, V. Lunch & dinner daily. Tube: Knightsbridge. Map p 96.*

★★★ **Gordon Ramsay** CHELSEA
FRENCH Its three Michelin stars are no joke: This is serious haute cuisine at its best, and dedicated gastronomes find it worth every pound. *68 Royal Hospital Rd.* ☎ *0207/352-4441. www.gordonramsay.com. Set lunch £40, dinner £70. AE, DC, MC, V. Lunch & dinner Mon–Fri. Tube: Sloane Sq. Map p 96.*

★ **kids HK Diner** SOHO *CHINESE*
The no-frills Cantonese food is a big hit with the after-club set when they need a nosh at 3am. *22 Wardour St.* ☎ *0207/287-9566. Entrees £8–£20. MC, V. Lunch & dinner daily. Tube: Piccadilly. Map p 98.*

★★ **kids Itsu** SOUTH KENSINGTON
ASIAN A fun place, where diners choose from an excellent selection of small but pricey dishes that roll by on a conveyor belt. *118 Draycott Ave.* ☎ *0207/590-2400. Dishes £5–£10. MC, V. Lunch & dinner daily. Tube: S. Kensington. Map p 96.*

★★ **The Ivy** SOHO *MODERN BRITISH* The menu is surprisingly diverse (ranging from caviar to fish cakes to irresistible puddings) at this exclusive haunt of British celebs. For a fancy place, it's not terribly overpriced. *1 West St.* ☎ *0207/836-4751. Entrees £10–£24. AE, DC, MC, V. Lunch & dinner daily. Tube: Leicester Sq. Map p 98.*

★★ **kids Jakob's** KENSINGTON
MIDDLE EASTERN A big hit with locals, this deli-style restaurant provides healthy, home-cooked meals at a fair price. *20 Gloucester Rd.* ☎ *0207/581-9292. Entrees £6–£10. AE, MC, V. Breakfast, lunch & dinner Mon–Sat; breakfast & lunch Sun. Tube: Gloucester Rd. Map p 96.*

★★ **kids Joe Allen** SOHO *AMERICAN* A good post-theater place for more than the usual burgers and steaks. There's a pianist and great pecan pie. Open late. *13 Exeter St.* ☎ *0207/836-0651. Entrees £10–£20. AE, MC, V. Lunch & dinner daily. Tube: Covent Garden. Map p 98.*

★★ **Kensington Place** KENSINGTON *MODERN BRITISH* Come here for innovative fresh fish dishes served in a modern, noisy dining room. *201 Kensington Church St.* ☎ *0207/727-3184. Entrees £10–£23. AE, DC, MC, V. Lunch & dinner daily. Tube: Notting Hill. Map p 96.*

★★ **kids Langan's Brasserie**
ST. JAMES *BRASSERIE* A big upscale brasserie with two noisy floors of

You can't leave London without trying the city's famous fish-and-chips.

A sampling of the French haute cuisine served at the renowned Le Gavroche.

dining, serving everything from spinach soufflé to fish-and-chips. *Stratton St.* ☎ *0207/491-8822. Entrees £10–£20. AE, DC, MC, V. Lunch & dinner Mon–Fri; dinner Sat. Tube: Green Park. Map p 98.*

★★ kids **Le Brasserie** SOUTH KENSINGTON *BRASSERIE* It's almost like eating in a Parisian cafe (you'll find *coq au vin* and other brasserie standards), but more costly. *Le petit dejeuner, le dejeuner, et le diner* served *avec* panache. *272 Brompton Rd.* ☎ *0207/581-3089. Entrees £8–£17. AE, DC, MC, V. Breakfast, lunch & dinner daily. Tube: S. Kensington. Map p 96.*

★★★ **Le Gavroche** MAYFAIR *FRENCH* Internationally renowned chef Michel Roux oversees the kitchen at this Michelin three-star extravaganza serving classic French haute cuisine in a clubby, elegant dining room. *43 Upper Brook St.* ☎ *0207/408-0881. £40 prix-fixe lunch, £78 tasting menu. AE, DC, MC, V. Lunch & dinner Mon–Fri; dinner Sat. Tube: Marble Arch. Map p 98.*

★★★ **Lindsay House** SOHO *MODERN BRITISH* Richard Corrigan, one of London's most inventive chefs,

uses French and Irish techniques to create English culinary wonders in a beautiful Regency dining room. There's a good wine list. *21 Romilly St.* ☎ *0207/439-0450. Set menu £25–£62. AE, DC, MC, V. Lunch & dinner Mon–Fri; dinner Sat. Tube: Piccadilly. Map p 98.*

★★ kids **Marouch V** MARYLEBONE *MIDDLE EASTERN* This branch of a popular London chain, well known for its good value, offers a big menu that includes fresh-squeezed juices and excellent falafel. Open late. *4 Vere St.* ☎ *0207/493-3030. Entrees £8–£12. AE, DC, MC, V. Breakfast, lunch & dinner daily. Tube: Bond St. Map p 98.*

★★★ kids **Mildred's** SOHO *VEGETARIAN* The best vegetarian/vegan restaurant in London serves well-priced health food faves such as stir-fries, veggie burgers, salads, and juices. Don't skip the tasty desserts. *45 Lexington St.* ☎ *0207/494-1634. Entrees £6–£8. No credit cards. Lunch & dinner daily. Tube: Piccadilly. Map p 98.*

★★★ kids **Momo** MAYFAIR *MOROCCAN* Decorated in Arabian Nights splendor, this West End success story is a wonderful place for a taste of exotic and fantastic *tagines* (a Morroccan spiced stew)! *25 Heddon St.* ☎ *0207/434-4040. Entrees £10–£20. AE, DC, MC, V. Lunch & dinner daily. Tube: Oxford Circus. Map p 98.*

★ kids **My Old Dutch Pancake House** CHELSEA *CREPERIE* Stick to the thin pancakes, which are as large as a pizza and topped with whatever you fancy. *221 King's Rd.* ☎ *0207/376-5650. Entrees £5–£8. AE, MC, V. Breakfast, lunch & dinner daily. Tube: Sloane Sq. Map p 96.*

★★★ **Nobu** MAYFAIR *JAPANESE/ FUSION* Known for its glamour (via owner Robert de Niro), its staggering tabs, and its creative sushi. *Metropolitan Hotel, 19 Old Park Lane.* ☎ *0207/376-5650. Entrees £15–£20. AE, MC, V. Lunch & dinner Mon–Fri noon–2pm; dinner Sat–Sun. Tube: Hyde Park Corner. Map p 98.*

★★★ **kids Orsini's Cafe** SOUTH KENSINGTON *ITALIAN* Opposite the V&A, this cafe right out of Naples features great daily specials, perfectly prepared pastas, and the best cappuccino around. *8a Thurloe Place.* ☎ *0207/581-5553. Entrees £6–£9. AE, MC, V. Breakfast, lunch & dinner daily. Tube: S. Kensington. Map p 96.*

★★ **Oxo Tower Brasserie** SOUTHBANK *GLOBAL FUSION* Get the best river views in London while dining on a somewhat pricey menu of dishes that combine Mediterranean, French, and Asian ingredients. The 1930s-style dining room is quite chic, but you should dine on the balcony in summer. *Oxo Tower Wharf, Bargehouse St.* ☎ *0207/803-3888. Entrees £10–£20. AE, DC, MC, V. Lunch & dinner daily. Tube: Blackfriars. Map p 95.*

Nobu's creative sushi attracts a glamorous crowd.

★ **kids Patisserie Valerie** KENSINGTON *CAFE* Visit this popular cafe for its addictive croissants, reasonable lunches, and incredible pastries. The Parisian-flavored Belle Epoque decor only adds to its charm. *27 Kensington Church St.* ☎ *0207/937-9574. Entrees £5–£10. AE, MC, V. Breakfast, lunch & dinner daily. Tube: Kensington High St. Map p 96.*

★★ **kids The People's Palace** SOUTH BANK *MODERN BRITISH* Spectacular city views mix with modern British cuisine at a restaurant located just off Thames Walk near the London Eye (combine a ride and a two-course meal for just £28). *Level 3, Royal Festival Hall.* ☎ *0207/928-9999. Entrees £15–£20. AE, DC, MC, V. Lunch & dinner daily. Tube: Waterloo. Map p 95.*

★★ **kids Pizza on the Park** KNIGHTSBRIDGE *PIZZA/ITALIAN* Live jazz makes this pizza joint more attractive than all its brethren in the city. *11–13 Knightsbridge.* ☎ *0207/ 235-5273. Entrees £8–£15. AE, DC, MC, V. Breakfast, lunch & dinner daily. Tube: Hyde Park Corner. Map p 96.*

★★★ **Poisonnerie de l'Avenue** SOUTH KENSINGTON *FRENCH/ SEAFOOD* A very old-school yet very friendly place, with impeccable service, excellent fish, and creative French-influenced dishes (try the brochette of monkfish). *82 Sloane Ave.* ☎ *0207/589-2457. Entrees £13–£25. AE, DC, MC, V. Lunch & dinner daily. Tube: S. Kensington. Map p 96.*

★ **kids Porters English Restaurant** COVENT GARDEN *TRADITIONAL BRITISH* The Earl of Bradford's eatery serves simple and traditional English food in the heart of Theaterland. The comfortable two-story restaurant is family-friendly, informal, and lively. Check www.porters.uk. com for theater-and-dinner deals.

A traditional English breakfast.

17 Henrietta St. ☎ 0207/836-6466. Entrees £10–£16. AE, MC, V. Lunch & dinner daily. Tube: Charing Cross. Map p 98.

★ **The Portrait** SOHO *MODERN BRITISH* The big attraction here is the gorgeous view over Trafalgar Square, but the food—ranging from chargrilled Scottish sirloin to baked cod—is tasty, too. The excellent wine list features some organic vintages. *The National Portrait Gallery, St. Martin's Lane.* ☎ 0207/312-2490. Entrees £10–£17. AE, DC, MC, V. Lunch daily; dinner Thurs–Fri. Tube: Charing Cross. Map p 98.

★ **kids The Providores and Tapa Room** MARYLEBONE *GLOBAL* The Tapa Room features savory breakfasts; head upstairs to the restaurant for interesting twists on global favorites. *109 Marylebone High St.* ☎ 0207/935-6175. Entrees £8–£17. AE, MC, V. Tapa Room: Breakfast, lunch & dinner daily. Restaurant: Lunch & dinner daily. Tube: Bond St. Map p 98.

★★ **Racine** KNIGHTSBRIDGE *FRENCH* For unpretentious and flavorful cuisine, served by a

professional staff in a classy setting, try this popular bistro. *239 Brompton Rd.* ☎ 0207/584-4477. Entrees £12–£20. AE, MC, V. Lunch & dinner daily. Tube: Knightsbridge. Map p 96.

★ **kids Rainforest Café** SOHO *AMERICAN* It's not a meal, it's a safari loaded with foliage and animatronic animals. Head to this non-smoking and kid-pleasing joint for the atmosphere, though the food isn't bad. *20–24 Shaftsbury Ave.* ☎ 0207/434-3111. Entrees £10–£16. AE, DC, MC, V. Lunch & dinner daily. Tube: Piccadilly. Map p 98.

★★★ **The Ritz Palm Court** WEST END *ENGLISH TEA* Women, wear your best dress to this very deluxe (and pricey!) tea, served in a Versailles-like setting. Book well in advance. *150 Piccadilly.* ☎ 0207/493-8181. £68 for 2. AE, DC, MC, V. Afternoon tea daily. Tube: Green Park. Map p 98.

★★ **Rules** COVENT GARDEN *TRADITIONAL ENGLISH* The most traditional Olde English restaurant in London, Rules dates back to 1798, and is a must for Anglophiles and

For traditional British cuisine, you can't do much better than Rules.

lovers of roast beef and Yorkshire pudding. *35 Maiden Lane.* ☎ *0207/836-5314. Entrees £10–£20. AE, MC, V. Lunch & dinner daily. Tube: Charing Cross. Map p 98.*

★★ **San Lorenzo** KNIGHTSBRIDGE *ITALIAN* Ladies who lunch and the local aristocracy love this celeb haunt, which serves simple dishes and yummy tiramisu. *22 Beauchamp Place.* ☎ *0207/584-1074. Entrees £10–£30. No credit cards. Lunch & dinner daily. Tube: Knightsbridge. Map p 96.*

★★★ **Savoy Grill** COVENT GARDEN *BRITISH* Known as "the second house of lords," the Grill is *the* power-lunch spot in London, and a sure bet for a fine meal with a view of the Thames. *Savoy Hotel, The Strand.* ☎ *0207/836-4343. Set lunch £30, set dinner £55. AE, MC, V. Lunch & dinner daily. Tube: Charing Cross. Map p 98.*

★★ **Tamarind** MAYFAIR *INDIAN* Diners ranging from business execs to couples appreciate this spot's elegant decor, and the imaginative menu that goes beyond the usual curries. *20 Queen St.* ☎ *0207/629-3561. Entrees £14–£22. AE, DC, MC, V. Lunch & dinner daily. Tube: Green Park. Map p 98.*

★ **kids** **Texas Embassy Cantina** SOHO *TEX MEX* Get knockout margaritas and a Wild West atmosphere in a historic building that once housed the owners of the *Titanic*. *1 Cockspur St.* ☎ *0207/925-0077. Entrees £8–£15. AE, MC, V. Lunch & dinner daily. Tube: Charing Cross. Map p 98.*

★ **kids** **Thai Pavilion** WEST END *THAI* A perfect location for pre-or post-theater pad-thai and other Thai specialties. *42 Rupert St.* ☎ *0207/287-6333. Entrees £8–£17. AE, DC, MC, V. Lunch & dinner daily. Tube: Piccadilly. Map p 98.*

★ **kids** **Vingt Quatre** CHELSEA *DINER* The best reason to come to this busy diner is that it's always open, serving blah brasserie food to jet-lagged insomniacs and after-hours clubbers. *325 Fulham Rd.* ☎ *0207/323-9223. Entrees £6–£15. MC, V. Open 24 hr. Tube: S. Kensington. Map p 96.*

★ **kids** **Wagamama** BLOOMSBURY *JAPANESE* You sit at large cafeteria-like tables where the noise level is considerable, but this popular Tokyo-style noodle chain is tops for reasonably priced Asian food. *4a Streatham St.* ☎ *0207/323-9223. Entrees £5–£15. AE, MC, V. Lunch & dinner daily. Tube: Tottenham Court. Map p 98.*

★★★ **The Wolseley Café Restaurant** ST. JAMES *ENGLISH* This stepsister of The Ivy, set in a high-ceilinged Art Deco dining room, dishes out celeb sightings and a large menu offering decent value. And it serves breakfast! *160 Piccadilly.* ☎ *0207/499-6996. www.thewolseley.com. Entrees £10–£30. AE, DC, MC, V. Breakfast, lunch & dinner daily. Tube: Green Park. Map p 98.* ●

Nightlife Best Bets

Most **Divine in Every Way**
★★★ Heaven, *Under the Arches,
Villiers St.* (p 120)

Most **Diverse Entertainment**
★★★ Madame JoJo's, *8–10 Brewer
St.* (p 120)

Best **Jazz Club**
★★★ Ronnie Scott's, *47 Frith St.*
(p 121)

Most **Decadent Decor**
★★★ Opium, *1A Dean St.* (p 121)

Best **Club to Wear Your
Bathing Suit to**
★★★ Aquarium, *256 Old St.* (p 119)

Most **Unpretentious**
★★ Plastic People, *147–149 Curtain
Rd.* (p 121)

Best **Name**
★★ Filthy McNasty's, *68 Amwell St.*
(p 118)

Best **Views**
★★★ Vertigo 42, *25 Old Broad St.*
(p 119)

Best **Historic Pub**
★★★ Ye Olde Cheshire Cheese,
145 Fleet St. (p 123)

Best **for Blues**
★★ Ain't Nothin' But? The Blues
Bar, *20 Kingly St.* (p 117)

Ronnie Scott's, London's best jazz club.

Most **Elegant Pub/Bar**
★★ Old Bank of England,
94 Fleet St. (p 116); or ★★★ The
Crosse Keys, *9 Gracechurch St.*
(p 124)

Best **Dance Club**
★★ Herbal, *12–14 Kingsland Rd.*
(p 120)

Best **Place to Spot a Celeb**
★★★ The Social, *5 Little Portland
St.* (p 121)

Best **Sports Bar**
★★ Sports Café, *80 Haymarket*
(p 119)

Best **Gay Bar**
★★★ The Edge, *11 Soho Sq.* (p 118)

Best **Cocktail Lounge**
★★ Blue Bar, *Berkeley Hotel, Wilton
Place* (p 117)

Best **Hotel Bar**
★★★ The Library, *Laneborough
Hotel, Hyde Park Corner* (p 118)

Best **Dressed Crowd**
★★ Isola, *145 Knightsbridge* (p 118)

Best **Cocktails**
★★★ BBar, *43 Buckingham Palace
Rd.* (p 117)

Most **Romantic**
★★★ Windows Bar, *London Hilton,
22 Park Lane* (p 119)

Best **Club for Singles**
★★★ Fabric, *77A Charterhouse St.*
(p 120)

Best **People-Watching**
★★ Purple Bar at The Sanderson,
50 Berners St. (p 118)

Best **Bloody Marys**
★★ The Grenadier, *18 Wilton Row*
(p 115)

Best **Bohemian Hangout**
★★ Troubadour Café, *265 Old
Brompton Rd.* (p 116)

Notting Hill Nightlife

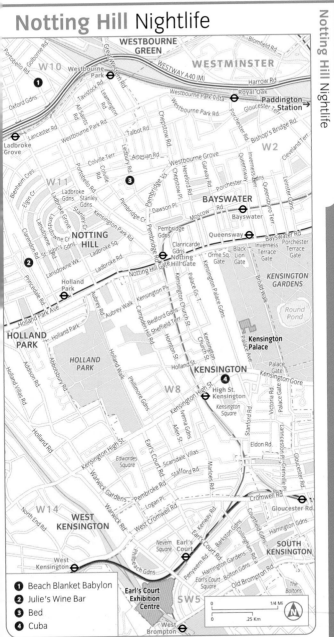

1 Beach Blanket Babylon
2 Julie's Wine Bar
3 Bed
4 Cuba

West End Nightlife

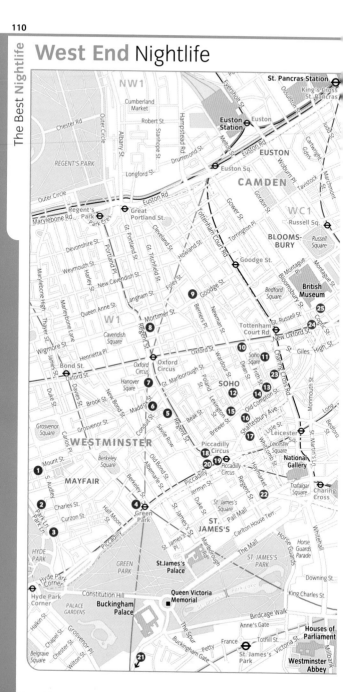

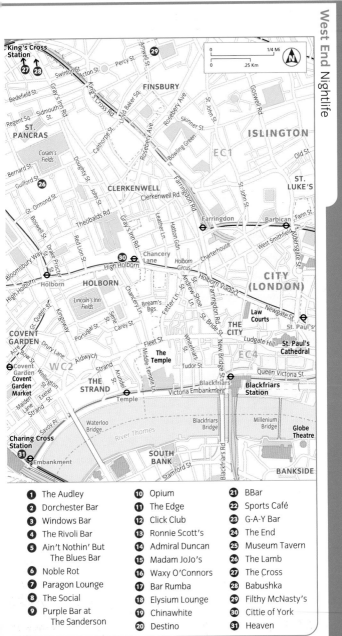

1. The Audley
2. Dorchester Bar
3. Windows Bar
4. The Rivoli Bar
5. Ain't Nothin' But The Blues Bar
6. Noble Rot
7. Paragon Lounge
8. The Social
9. Purple Bar at The Sanderson
10. Opium
11. The Edge
12. Click Club
13. Ronnie Scott's
14. Admiral Duncan
15. Madam JoJo's
16. Waxy O'Connors
17. Bar Rumba
18. Elysium Lounge
19. Chinawhite
20. Destino
21. BBar
22. Sports Café
23. G-A-Y Bar
24. The End
25. Museum Tavern
26. The Lamb
27. The Cross
28. Babushka
29. Filthy McNasty's
30. Cittie of York
31. Heaven

Chelsea Nightlife

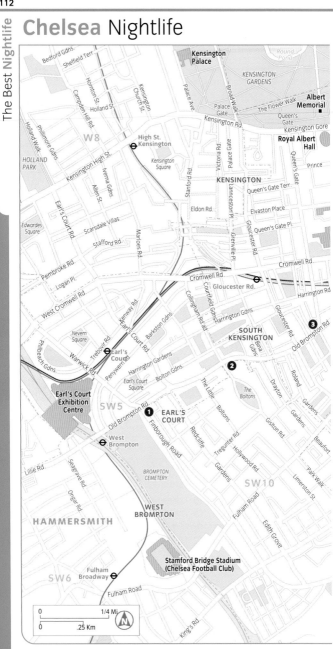

Kensington Palace

KENSINGTON GARDENS

Round Pond

Albert Memorial

The Flower Walk

Queen's Gate

Kensington Gore

Royal Albert Hall

Prince

Palace Gate

Kensington Rd.

KENSINGTON

Queen's Gate Terr.

Elvaston Place

Queen's Gate Pl.

Cromwell Rd.

Harrington Rd.

Gloucester Rd.

SOUTH KENSINGTON

❸ Old Brompton Rd.

❷

❶ EARL'S COURT

Earl's Court

West Brompton

BROMPTON CEMETERY

SW10

WEST BROMPTON

HAMMERSMITH

Stamford Bridge Stadium (Chelsea Football Club)

Fulham Broadway

Fulham Road

SW6

King's Rd.

Bedford Gdns.

Sheffield Terr.

Hornton St.

Holland St.

Camden Hill Rd.

Kensington Church St.

Palace Ave.

Broad Walk

Palace Gate

Victoria Rd.

Palace Gate

W8

High St. Kensington

Kensington Square

Lancaster Pl.

Grenville Pl.

Gloucester Rd.

Phillimore Gdns.

Holland Walk

HOLLAND PARK

Kensington High St.

Iverna Gdns.

Allen St.

Stanford Rd.

Eldon Rd.

Earl's Court Rd.

Scarsdale Villas

Marloes Rd.

Edwardes Square

Stafford Rd.

Pembroke Rd.

Logan Pl.

West Cromwell Rd.

Nevern Square

Philbeach Gdns.

Warwick Rd.

Trebovir Rd.

Penywern Rd.

Earl's Court Rd.

Kenway Rd.

Barkston Gdns.

Courtfield Gdns.

Collingham Rd.

Harrington Gdns.

Harrington Gardens

Bolton Gdns.

The Little Boltons

The Boltons

Bina Gdns.

Roland Gardens

Drayton Gardens

Gilston Rd.

Beaufort

Earl's Court Square

Earl's Court Exhibition Centre

SW5

Old Brompton Rd.

Finborough Road

Redcliffe Gardens

Tregunter Rd.

Hollywood Rd.

Limerston St.

Park Walk

Lillie Rd.

Seagrave Rd.

Ongar Rd.

Edith Grove

Fulham Road

0   1/4 Mi.

0   .25 Km

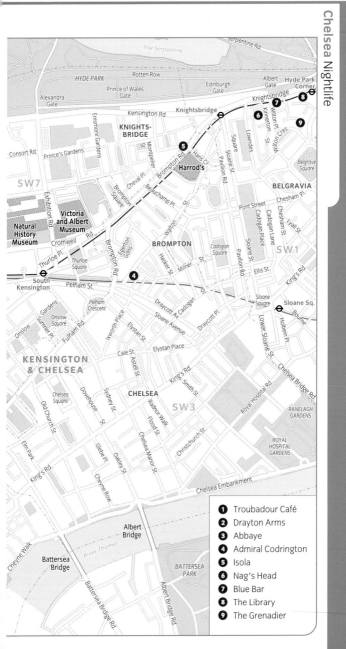

1. Troubadour Café
2. Drayton Arms
3. Abbaye
4. Admiral Codrington
5. Isola
6. Nag's Head
7. Blue Bar
8. The Library
9. The Grenadier

Nightlife in **The City**

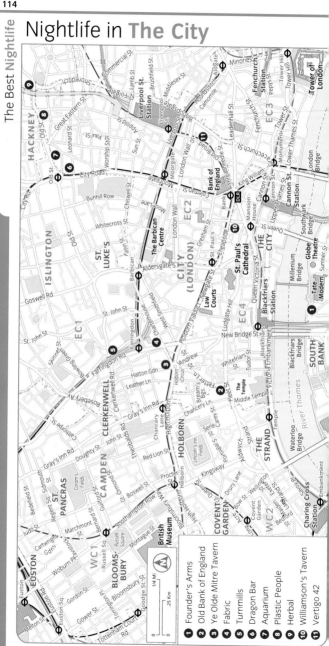

1. Founder's Arms
2. Old Bank of England
3. Ye Olde Mitre Tavern
4. Fabric
5. Turnmills
6. Dragon Bar
7. Aquarium
8. Plastic People
9. Herbal
10. Williamson's Tavern
11. Vertigo 42

London Nightlife A to Z

Pubs

★★ Admiral Codrington

CHELSEA   This cozy and attractive pub features a friendly staff, good food, a well-heeled crowd from neighboring Chelsea and South Kensington, and outdoor tables that handle overflow on warm evenings. *17 Mossup St. ☎ 0207/581-0005. Tube: S. Kensington. Map p 112.*

★★ Admiral Duncan SOHO

This old standard weathered a homophobe's bomb in 1999, and now offers bargain shots and unusually dim lighting. Gay or straight, it's a mellow and friendly place to drink. *54 Old Compton St. ☎ 0207/437-5300. Tube: Leicester Sq. Map p 110.*

★★★ The Audley MAYFAIR   This

is one of London's more beautiful old-school pubs, evocative of a Victorian-era gentlemen's club (it was built in the 1880s). Slip into a booth beneath the original chandeliers and sample the traditional English grub. *41 Mount St. ☎ 0207/499-1843. Tube: Green Park. Map p 110.*

★★★ Cittie of York BLOOMSBURY

There's been a pub on this site since

The mellow Admiral Duncan is a friendly place to down a pint.

1430, and though the current building dates back to the 1890s, there's still an old-world (faux) vibe, and (real) ale. Check out the churchlike interior and its immense wine vats. Closed Sunday. *22 High Holborn. ☎ 0207/242-7670. Tube: Chancery Lane. Map p 110.*

★★ Drayton Arms EARL'S COURT

Raise a pint with the friendly patrons crowding the wide-open interiors of this historic pub (a lot of the building's original architectural features are still present). There's outdoor seating when the weather's fine. *153 Old Brompton Rd. ☎ 0207/835-2301. Tube: Earl's Court. Map p 112.*

★★ Founder's Arms SOUTH

BANK   This great summer-only pub, built on the site of a foundry near the Tate Modern, is neither old nor authentic. It does, however, offer good value and wonderful views of St. Paul's and the Millennium Bridge. *52 Hopton St. ☎ 0207/928-1899. Tube: Blackfriars. Map p 114.*

★★ The Grenadier BELGRAVIA

This charming pub is tucked in a secluded mews. It's best known for its Sunday bloody marys, resident ghost, and historic military past (the Duke of Wellington's soldiers used it as their mess hall). *18 Wilton Row. ☎ 0207/235-3074. Tube: Knightsbridge. Map p 112.*

★★ The Lamb BLOOMSBURY

You'll find one of the city's few remaining "snob screens"—used to protect drinkers from prying eyes—at this Victorian pub. Those who've enjoyed the anonymity here include the Bloomsbury Group and Charles Dickens. *98 Lamb's Conduit St. ☎ 0207/405-0713. Tube: Russell Sq. Map p 110.*

★★ **Museum Tavern** BLOOMS-BURY   This early-18th-century (and marketing-savvy) pub, the former Dog & Duck, changed its name when the British Museum was built across the street in the 1760s. The old-style decor remains intact. *49 Great Russell St.* ☎ *0207/242-8987. Tube: Russell Sq. Map p 110.*

★★★ **Nags Head** BELGRAVIA   This rarity, an independently owned pub, was built in the early 19th century for the posh area's working stiffs. A "no cellphones" rule keeps the 21st century from intruding. *53 Kinnerton St.* ☎ *0207/235-1135. Tube: Knightsbridge. Map p 112.*

★★ **Old Bank of England** THE CITY   This unusual pub is housed in a converted former bank that has retained all the majesty of a palace of finance, with a huge interior and wonderful murals. It's a City hangout, so it's closed on weekends. *194 Fleet St.* ☎ *0207/430-2255. Tube: Temple. Map p 114.*

★★ **Troubadour Café** EARL'S COURT   Yes, it's a restaurant, but it's also a pub, a bar, and a bohemian hangout. There are poetry readings, live music, and singer-songwriter nights. *265 Old Brompton Rd.*

☎ *0207/370-1434. www.troubadour. co.uk. Tube: Earl's Court. Map p 112.*

★★ **Williamson's Tavern** EAST END   With a history that goes back to Londinium (there are excavated Roman tiles in the fireplace), this pub was once the home of the Lord Mayor of London and lies in an alley fronted by gates that were gifts of William III and Mary II. *1 Groveland Court.* ☎ *0207/248-6280. Tube: Mansion House. Map p 114.*

★★★ **Ye Olde Mitre Tavern** EAST END   Good service, beamed ceilings, and the stump of a tree Queen Elizabeth I reportedly frolicked under, make this historic treasure a must-see. It's hard to find, but do try. *Ely Court, off Ely Place.* ☎ *0207/405-4751. Tube: Chancery Lane. Map p 114.*

Bars
★★ **Abbaye** SOUTH KENSINGTON   A mellow atmosphere and some truly outstanding beers make this European brasserie and bar a great hangout. Wash down some mussels with the great Belgian suds. *102 Old Brompton Rd.* ☎ *0207/373-2403. Tube: Gloucester Rd. Map p 112.*

The old-fashioned Nags Head in Belgravia.

★★ Ain't Nothin' But? The Blues Bar SOHO A blues joint plucked straight from the bayou; it may not be Bourbon Street, but there's good jambalaya, funky tables, and a variety of fine bluesmen (and women). Be prepared to wait in line on weekends. *20 Kingly St.* ☎ *0207/287-0514. Cover £5. Tube: Piccadilly Circus. Map p 110.*

★★ Babushka ISLINGTON Seasonal outdoor tables and a vaguely Russian decor contribute to the warm charm of this bar—a comfy place to relax and knock back flavored vodka drinks. DJs spin tunes on weekends. *125 Caledonian Rd.* ☎ *0207/837-1924. www.styleinthecity.co.uk. Tube: King's Cross. Map p 110.*

★ Beach Blanket Babylon KENSINGTON Truly wacko decor (a fireplace shaped like a tiger's mouth, a gangplank, and other kitschy excesses) will bring a smile to your lips that the often lousy service won't entirely wipe off. *45 Ledbury Rd.* ☎ *0207/229-2907. Tube: Notting Hill Gate. Map p 109.*

★★★ BBar VICTORIA A wicked cocktail menu (54 in all!), superior nibbles, and a vast wine cellar make this relaxed bar with an Africa-inspired decor a good place to drink. *43 Buckingham Palace Rd.* ☎ *0207/958-7000. www.bbarlondon.com. Tube: Victoria. Map p 110.*

★★ Bed NOTTING HILL Music mixes spun by accomplished DJs combine with specialty cocktails to induce a relaxed euphoria in this shabby-chic Moroccan-flavored oasis. *310 Portobello Rd.* ☎ *0208/969-4500. www.styleinthecity.co.uk. Tube: Ladbroke Grove. Map p 109.*

★★ Blue Bar KNIGHTSBRIDGE In the lovely Berkeley Hotel, this tiny (50-person) and, yes, blue (Luyten's blue, to be exact) bar serves 50

Down a whisky at the Berkeley Hotel's elegant Blue Bar.

varieties of whisky and tapas-type snacks to a very upscale crowd. *The Berkeley Hotel, Wilton Place.* ☎ *0207/235-6000. Tube: Hyde Park Corner. Map p 112.*

★★ Cuba KENSINGTON It's small, it's atmospheric, and with all the photos on the wall of Fidel and Che, you know it's Cuban. Salsa (they offer dance lessons), piña coladas, and lots of Latin men make for a good time. *11–13 Kensington High St.* ☎ *0207/938-4137. Tube: High St. Kensington. Map p 109.*

★★★ Dorchester Bar MAYFAIR It's hard to say if this hotel bar is really elegant or really corny, but you've got to see Liberace's rhinestone piano played along with live jazz on Wednesday and Sunday nights. *53 Park Lane.* ☎ *0207/629-8888. Tube: Hyde Park Corner. Map p 110.*

★ Dragon Bar ISLINGTON This funky down-home kind of place is too hip to put its name over the door (it's engraved on the entrance steps, so look down). There's a fireplace in the winter, beat-up leather couches, good DJs, and an arty young crowd. *5 Leonard St.* ☎ *0207/490-7110. Tube: Angel. Map p 114.*

Sip a cocktail at The Library bar in the posh Lanesborough hotel.

★★★ **The Edge** SOHO   Take the edge off your day at this classy, entertaining gay and lesbian club, which caters to a diverse crowd with a cafe, piano bar, lounge, dance floor, and plenty of colorful characters. *11 Soho Sq.* ☎ *0207/439-1313. www.edge.uk.com. Tube: Tottenham Court Rd. Map p 110.*

★★ **Filthy McNasty's** KING'S CROSS   Wonderful pub fun, with waiters whose uniforms are in disarray and a genial attitude of "Who gives a toss?" Weekends offer live music on the back stage, and poetry readings every other Sunday. *68 Amwell St.* ☎ *0207/837-6067. Tube: Angel. Map p 110.*

★★★ **G-A-Y Bar** SOHO   In the center of Old Compton Street's "Gaysville," three floors filled with video screens and pop music cater to people of every sexual persuasion looking for fun. *30 Old Compton St.* ☎ *0207/494-2756. Tube: Leicester Sq. Map p 110.*

★★ **Isola** KNIGHTSBRIDGE   This upscale bar above the Oliver Peyton restaurant in Knightsbridge features floor-to-ceiling windows, well-dressed women, a decent wine list, and strong cocktails. *145 Knightsbridge.* ☎ *0207/838-1044. Tube: Knightsbridge. Map p 112.*

★★ **Julie's Wine Bar** HOLLAND PARK   The lovely little wine bar has reasonably good food and a charming atmosphere. It's surrounded by an assortment of intriguing shops. *137 Portland St.* ☎ *0207/727-7985. www.juliesrestaurant.com. Tube: Holland Park. Map p 109.*

★★★ **The Library** KNIGHTS-BRIDGE   Lots of business execs on expense accounts sip cocktails and cognac at this sophisticated and atmospheric bar in the Lanesborough hotel. A roaring fire and tinkling piano keys complete the picture. *1 Lanesborough Place.* ☎ *0207/259-5599. Tube: Hyde Park Corner. Map p 112.*

★★ **Noble Rot** MAYFAIR   Although it becomes a members-only club after 10pm, come here for dinner and you might get to stay for the stylish bar scene, featuring a Who's Who of posh young London. *3–5 Mill St.* ☎ *0207/626-8878. www. noblerot.com. Tube: Oxford Circus. Map p 110.*

★★ **Purple Bar at The Sanderson** SOHO   In the achingly hip and visually modern Sanderson Hotel, this intimate bar is draped in all shades of purple, beautifully lit, and terribly expensive. Sip a martini and people-watch. *50 Berners St.* ☎ *0207/300-1444. Tube: Goodge St. Map p 110.*

★★★ **The Rivoli Bar** WEST END   The Ritz Hotel's restored Art Deco bar offers all the atmosphere you would expect of a bastion of over-the-top swank, as well as a varied menu of expensive drinks. A strict dress code keeps the young at bay. *150 Piccadilly.* ☎ *0207/493-8181. Tube: Green Park. Map p 110.*

★★ Sports Café WEST END
When you've got to get your sports fix, this is the place to come: 120 TVs, seven pool tables, three bars, a dance floor, and four giant screens of games, games, and more games. *80 Haymarket.* ☎ *0207/839-8300. Tube: Piccadilly Circus. Map p 110.*

★★★ Vertigo 42 THE CITY
On the 42nd floor of a skyscraper, this bar is the highest in England and features splendid (and rare for London) views. It's the perfect place to sip a cocktail at sunset. *Tower 42, 25 Old Broad St.* ☎ *0207/877-7842. www.vertigo42.co.uk. Tube: Liverpool St. Map p 114.*

★ Waxy O'Connors WEST END
This roaring Irish bar features mad Gaelic music, tipsy crowds, and a shameless sort of tourist appeal. The weird decor improves with each drink—you'll love the indoor tree. *14–16 Rupert St.* ☎ *0207/287-0255. www.waxyoconnors.co.uk. Tube: Leicester Sq. Map p 110.*

★★★ Windows Bar MAYFAIR
The best view of Hyde Park to be had is from this very chi-chi bar on the 28th floor of the London Hilton on Park Lane. Dress is strictly smart casual, and a selection of fine cigars is available. *22 Park Lane.* ☎ *0207/ 493-8000. www.hilton.co.uk. Tube: Hyde Park Corner. Map p 110.*

Dance Clubs and Live Music
★★★ Aquarium EAST END
This crazy but popular nightclub offers you the chance to doff your clothes and jump in a pool with strangers.

Germaphobes may want to stick to the fully clothed drinking and dancing. *256 Old St.* ☎ *0207/251-6136. www.clubaquarium.co.uk. £8–£15 cover. Tube: Old St. Map p 114.*

★★★ Bar Rumba SOHO
Ten years of late nights haven't taken the blush off Bar Rumba, with its great resident musicians, live jazz, salsa, house, two dance floors, and kickin' cocktails. *36 Shaftsbury Ave.* ☎ *0207/287-6933. www.barrumba. co.uk. £3–£12 cover after 9pm. Tube: Leicester Sq. Map p 110.*

★ Chinawhite WEST END
Though well past its white-hot hipness of the '90s, this sexy and opulent club has a small dance floor and a vigilant velvet rope policy—though you can get in if the door staff likes your look. *6 Air St.* ☎ *0207/343-0040. www.chinawhite.com. £10–£20 cover. Tube: Piccadilly. Map p 110.*

★★ Click Club SOHO
Hilariously tacky Hollywood decor, exotic cocktails, and loud music for the young set. *84 Wardour St.* ☎ *0207/734-5447. £10 cover. Call ahead to be put on guest list. Tube: Piccadilly. Map p 110.*

★★★ The Cross KING'S CROSS
This club's outdoor garden is a great escape from the three dance floors heaving with ravers till 6am. A huge venue with lots of little rooms. *27–31 York Way.* ☎ *0207/837-0828. www.the-cross.co.uk. £12–£15 cover. Tube: King's Cross. Map p 110.*

★★★ Destino MAYFAIR
There are three floors of fun at this former restaurant, "Down Mexico Way." It's still got the spicy food, but the emphasis is now on dancing and drinking tequila while surrounded by antique tiles. *25 Swallow St.* ☎ *0207/437-9895. £10–£20 cover. Tube: Piccadilly. Map p 110.*

The London Hilton's Windows Bar offers a phenomenal view of the city.

★★ Elysium Lounge WEST END

Its Arabian Nights decor and small dance floor date it a bit, and the drinks are pricey, but this club still blazes with beautiful people and is popular with the fashion industry set. Check for events and club nights. *68 Regent St.* ☎ *0207/439-7770. www.elysiumlounge.co.uk. £10–£20 cover. Tube: Piccadilly. Map p 110.*

★★★ The End BLOOMSBURY

The decor is all steel and glass, yet this club is completely comfortable. Very professional staff and an upbeat crowd, thanks to the amazing sound system. *18 W. Central St.* ☎ *0207/419-9199. www.endclub.com. Tickets £8–£20 (book ahead). Tube: Tottenham Court Rd. Map p 110.*

★★★ Fabric EAST END

An immense weekend-only favorite, Fabric has a killer sound system and a bewildering number of dance floors and chill-out rooms full of potential new dance partners. This veteran never goes out of vogue with serious clubbers. *77a Charterhouse St.* ☎ *0207/336-8898. www.fabriclondon.com. £10–£15 cover. Tube: Farringdon. Map p 114.*

★★★ Heaven COVENT GARDEN

Proving no one does clubs better than gay revelers, this London landmark has 25 years of partying under its belt, and it's growing old disgracefully. *Under the Arches, Villiers St.* ☎ *0207/930-2020. www.heaven-london.com. £10–£20 cover. Tube: Embankment. Map p 110.*

★★ Herbal EAST END

In newly trendy Shoreditch, you'll find this dark and intimate club buzzing with two dance floors, the occasional celeb, and exotic music. Leave the suits at home; this is warehouse chic at its best. *12–14 Kingsland Rd.* ☎ *0207/613-4462. www.herbaluk.com. £5–£15 cover. Tube: Old St. Map p 114.*

★★★ Madame JoJo's SOHO

This unpretentious zone has a well-earned reputation as one of Soho's most fun clubs, with decent drink prices and a good dance floor. The nightly offerings range from live music to comedy to Saturday-night drag queens. *8–10 Brewer St.* ☎ *0207/734-3040. www.madamejojos.com. £5–£15 cover. Tube: Piccadilly. Map p 110.*

Heaven, a veteran London club, still packs in the crowds.

For a fun night of clubbing, head to Soho's Madame JoJo's.

★★★ Opium SOHO
This restaurant/club features a luxe French-Vietnamese interior and bizarre cocktails of exotic provenance, such as plantain-infused rum. Eclectic menu, live music, and a stylish, rich crowd. *1a Dean St.* ☎ *0207/287-9608. www.opium-bar-restaurant.com. £10–£15 cover. Tube: Tottenham Court Rd. Map p 110.*

★★ Paragon Lounge WEST END
Popular with the young and moneyed, this Art Deco nightclub features live music, dancing, and Italian food till the wee hours. *9 Hanover St.* ☎ *0207/355-3337. www.paragon lounge.co.uk. Tube: Oxford St. Map p 110.*

★★★ Plastic People EAST END
For true music aficionados, the decidedly unpretentious P.P. offers live jazz, Latin, techno, soul, hip-hop, house, and funk. Ironically named, it attracts a casual, jovial crowd. *147–149 Curtain Rd.* ☎ *0207/739-6471. www.plasticpeople.co.uk. £8–£15 cover. Tube: Old St. Map p 114.*

★★★ Ronnie Scott's SOHO
Open since 1959, this granddaddy of London's jazz clubs fully deserves its legendary reputation. The best jazz musicians in the world play this classy but relaxed venue every night. *47 Frith St.* ☎ *0207/439-0747. www.ronniescotts.co.uk. £10–£20 cover. Tube: Leicester Sq. Map p 110.*

★★★ The Social FITZROVIA
Civilized and unpretentious, this club hosts a casual, eclectic crowd, including the occasional celeb. Well-dressed dancers, an evening jukebox and late-night DJs, serious cocktails, and fun food. *5 Little Portland St.* ☎ *0207/636-4992. www.thesocial. com. Tube: Oxford Circus. Map p 110.*

★★★ Turnmills EAST END
Housed inside a mega-entertainment complex, this fantastic nightclub is a hit with the under-30 set, and features live music and top international DJs. Open very late. *63 Clerkenwell Rd.* ☎ *0207/250-3409. www.turnmills. com. £10–£20 cover. Tube: Farringdon. Map p 114.*

London **Pub Crawl**

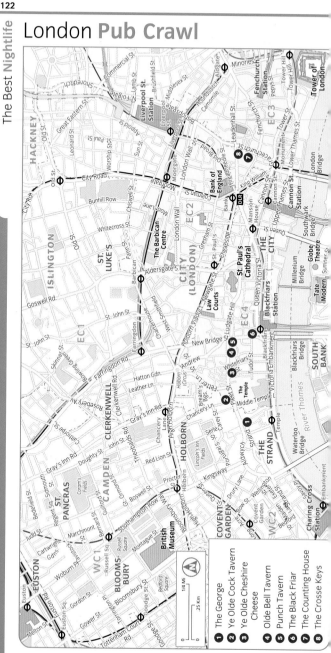

1 The George
2 Ye Olde Cock Tavern
3 Ye Olde Cheshire Cheese
4 Olde Bell Tavern
5 Punch Tavern
6 The Black Friar
7 The Counting House
8 The Crosse Keys

The public house, an institution that originated in London, was the place at the heart of a neighborhood where politics and gossip met with ale, beer, and coffee. Pubs doubled as post offices, inns, and gaming rooms, providing relaxation—and a chance to get rip-roaring drunk. Today's pubs still offer visitors a taste of the past along with a pint. This evening jaunt explores some of The City's best pubs and, like the intrepid explorers of the Empire, follows an eastward passage. START: **Temple Tube station**

1 ★★ The George. When it opened in 1723, it was a coffeehouse frequented by scribblers Horace Walpole, Oliver Goldsmith, and the ubiquitous Dr. Samuel Johnson. This traditional Victorian pub, set just across from the Royal Courts of Justice, still has beautiful if faux medieval timbering and stained glass. *213 The Strand.* ☎ *0207/353-9238. Map p 122.*

2 ★★ Ye Olde Cock Tavern. The main reason to come to this so-so pub is its architecture: The cockerel was supposedly made by master carver Grinling Gibbons, and much of the building survived the Great London Fire and dates back to the 16th century. It was a favorite of Dickens, Samuel Pepys, and Alfred Lord Tennyson (who mentioned it in one of his poems, a copy of which hangs near the entrance). Closed weekends. *22 Fleet St.* ☎ *0207/ 353-8570. Map p 122.*

The historic Ye Olde Cheshire Cheese is reportedly haunted.

In good weather, you can eat outside at The George.

3 ★★★ Ye Olde Cheshire Cheese. This wonderfully atmospheric, labyrinthine old pub was rebuilt right after the fire of 1666 and hasn't changed much since. Dr. Samuel Johnson lived around the corner, and other literary ghosts haunt the place. Closed weekends. *Wine Office Court, 145 Fleet St.* ☎ *0207/353-6170. Map p 122.*

4 ★★ Olde Bell Tavern. This cozy and authentic pub was built in the 1670s for the workmen constructing St. Bride's (the "wedding cake" church designed by Wren in 1670), and maintains an old-world ambience with its leaded windows and wainscoted walls. Its decor may not wow you, but this pub's laidback and genial atmosphere makes it a good spot for a pint. *95 Fleet St.* ☎ *0207/583-0216. Map p 122.*

The Black Friar pub was built on the site of a medieval monastery.

6 ★★★ **The Black Friar.** The amazingly detailed interior of this wedge-shaped Arts and Crafts pub is a feast for the eye. The magnificently carved friezes of monks remind you that the pub was built on the site of a 13th-century Dominican monastery, and under the vaulted ceiling you'll find such inscribed thoughts as WISDOM IS RARE. It's a popular after-work watering hole for The City's business set. *174 Queen Victoria St.* ☎ *0207/236-5650. Map p 122.*

7 ★★★ **The Counting House.** Oddly opulent despite its plain name, this must-see pub has a glass dome, a balcony (great for people-watching), extravagant chandeliers, gilded mirrors, and marbled walls. It looks more like a palace than a pub, but was actually a bank in a previous incarnation. *50 Cornhill St.* ☎ *0207/283-7123. Map p 122.*

5 ★★ **Punch Tavern.** Bearing the scars of an ownership feud that divided the premises in two, this Victorian pub was the place where *Punch* was founded in 1841; look for artifacts from that magazine (as well as *Punch & Judy*–themed memorabilia) on the walls. The bright interior features some beautifully etched mirrors and Art Nouveau chandeliers. *99 Fleet St.* ☎ *0207/353-6658. Map p 122.*

8 ★★★ **The Crosse Keys.** Very grand, this former bank is now an elegant pub with three separate eating rooms, a courtyard, high ceilings, wonderful wall carvings, and glass domes. It's almost too stately to be a pub, but then the best thing about London pubs is their crazy variety. *9 Gracechurch St.* ☎ *0207/623-4824. Map p 122.* ●

Welcome to
THE FAMOUS
PUNCH
TAVERN
ON
FLEET STREET

The historic Punch Tavern on Fleet Street.

9

The Best Arts & Entertainment

Arts & Entertainment
Best Bets

Best for a Laugh
★★★ Comedy Store, *17 Greek St.*
(p 130)

Best for Opera
★★★ Royal Opera House, *Covent Garden (p 131)*

Best Baroque Concerts
★★★ St. Martin-in-the-Fields Evening Candlelight Concerts, *Trafalgar Sq. (p 131)*

Best Restored Theater
★★★ Royal Albert Hall, *Kensington Gore (p 130)*

Most Comfortable Movie Theater Seats
★★ Chelsea Cinema, *206 King's Rd.*
(p 132)

Best for a Cheap Movie Date
★★★ Prince Charles Cinema, *7 Leicester Place (p 132)*

Best Cinema for the Whole Family
★★★ The Electric Cinema, *191 Portobello Rd. (p 132)*

Best Free Live-Music Performances
★★ St. James's Piccadilly, *197 Piccadilly (p 131)*

Best for Independent Films
★★ Curzon Mayfair, *38 Curzon St.*
(p 132)

Best Concert Venue
★★★ Barbican Centre, *Silk St.*
(p 130)

Best Outdoor Performances
★★ Open-Air Theatre, *Inner Circle, Regent's Park (p 133)*

Best Ballet
★★★ Sadler's Wells, *Rosebery Ave.*
(p 131)

The Criterion Theatre, home of the zany Reduced Shakespeare Company.

Best Symphony
★★★ London Symphony Orchestra at the Barbican Centre, *Silk St.*
(p 130)

Best Modern Dance
★★ The Place, *17 Duke's Rd. (p 131)*

Best Modern Theater
★★ Royal Court Theatre, *Sloane Sq. (p 133)*

Best Shakespeare
★★★ Shakespeare's Globe Theatre, *New Globe Walk (p 133)*

Best Theatrical Repertory Company
★★★ Royal National Theatre, *South Bank (p 133)*

Longest Running Drama
★★★ The Mousetrap, *St. Martin's Theatre (p 134)*

Longest Running Comedy
★★★ The Complete Works of William Shakespeare—Abridged, *The Criterion Theatre (p 134)*

West End **Theaters**

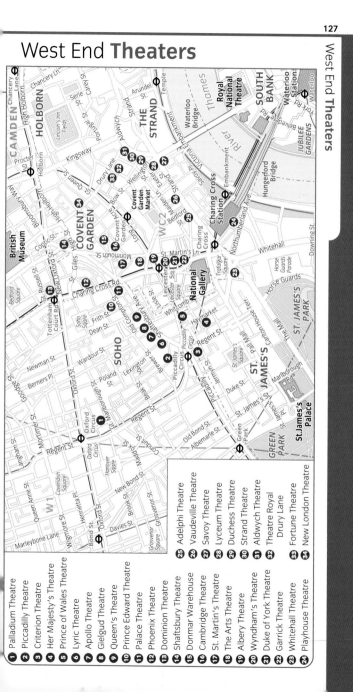

1. Palladium Theatre
2. Piccadilly Theatre
3. Criterion Theatre
4. Her Majesty's Theatre
5. Prince of Wales Theatre
6. Lyric Theatre
7. Apollo Theatre
8. Gielgud Theatre
9. Queen's Theatre
10. Prince Edward Theatre
11. Palace Theatre
12. Phoenix Theatre
13. Dominion Theatre
14. Shaftsbury Theatre
15. Donmar Warehouse
16. Cambridge Theatre
17. St. Martin's Theatre
18. The Arts Theatre
19. Albery Theatre
20. Wyndham's Theatre
21. Duke of York Theatre
22. Garrick Theatre
23. Whitehall Theatre
24. Playhouse Theatre
25. Adelphi Theatre
26. Vaudeville Theatre
27. Savoy Theatre
28. Lyceum Theatre
29. Duchess Theatre
30. Strand Theatre
31. Aldwych Theatre
32. Theatre Royal Drury Lane
33. Fortune Theatre
34. New London Theatre

London **Arts & Entertainment**

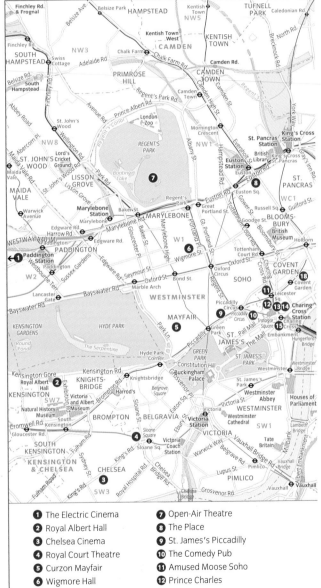

1. The Electric Cinema
2. Royal Albert Hall
3. Chelsea Cinema
4. Royal Court Theatre
5. Curzon Mayfair
6. Wigmore Hall
7. Open-Air Theatre
8. The Place
9. St. James's Piccadilly
10. The Comedy Pub
11. Amused Moose Soho
12. Prince Charles

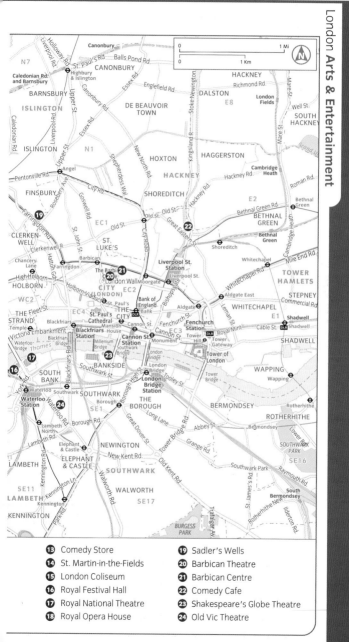

13 Comedy Store
14 St. Martin-in-the-Fields
15 London Coliseum
16 Royal Festival Hall
17 Royal National Theatre
18 Royal Opera House
19 Sadler's Wells
20 Barbican Theatre
21 Barbican Centre
22 Comedy Cafe
23 Shakespeare's Globe Theatre
24 Old Vic Theatre

Arts & Entertainment A to Z

Comedy

★★ Amused Moose Soho SOHO

Situated beneath a popular gay bar, this Thursday-through-Saturday comedy club has showcased such epic knee-slappers as Eddie Izzard. *Moonlighting, 17 Greek St.* ☎ *0207/341-1341. www.amusedmoose.co.uk. Tickets £9–£12. Tube: Leicester Sq. Map p 128.*

★★★ Comedy Cafe EAST END

Crowded tables and exposed brick walls provide an appropriate setting for raw comedy and plenty of heckling. There's a happy hour from 6 to 7pm. Closed Sunday to Tuesday. *66–68 Rivington St.* ☎ *0207/739-5706. www.comedycafe.fsnet.co.uk. Tickets free to £30. Tube: Old St. Map p 128.*

★★★ Comedy Store ST. JAMES

This veteran club has a proper stage and theater-style seating. It's less intimate than other clubs and the expensive drinks are nothing to laugh at, but it does feature the cream of the comedic crop. *1 Oxendon St.* ☎ *0207/7344-0234. www.thecomedystore.co.uk. £8–£15 cover. 2-drink minimum. Tube: Piccadilly. Map p 128.*

★★ The Comedy Pub SOHO

This late-night venue (till 2am) serves good pub food and features comedy duos, troupes, and occasionally bizarre comedic routines. Karaoke, too. *7 Oxendon St.* ☎ *0207/839-7261. Tickets £10. Tube: Piccadilly. Map p 128.*

Classical Music

★★★ Barbican Centre THE CITY

A gargantuan modern venue whose acoustics make it the best place for hearing music in the U.K. It's home to the first-class London Symphony Orchestra, which plays some 90

Royal Albert Hall hosts the Proms.

concerts here every year. *Silk St.* ☎ *0207/638-8891. www.barbican.org.uk. Tickets £5–£30. Tube: Barbican. Map p 128.*

★★ London Coliseum WEST END

Converted into an opera house in 1968, London's largest theater is home to the English National Opera. Productions range from Gilbert and Sullivan to more challenging modern fare; all are staged in English. *St. Martin's Lane.* ☎ *020/7632-8300. www.eno.org. Tickets £5–£78. Tube: Charing Cross. Map p 128.*

★★★ Royal Albert Hall

KENSINGTON This splendid Victorian pleasure palace is best known as the home of the city's annual Henry Wood Promenade Concerts (the Proms) in summer, when you'll hear orchestral classics and chamber music. *Kensington Gore.* ☎ *0207/589-8212. www.royalalberthall.com. Tickets £5–£70. Tube: Kensington High St. Map p 128.*

★★★ Royal Festival Hall SOUTH

BANK More than 150,000 hours of music have been performed at this acoustically exceptional complex since it opened in 1951. The hall's many free and low-priced concerts make it a great bet for those on a budget. *Belvedere Rd.* ☎ *0870/401-8181. www.rfh.org.uk. Tickets £6–£55. Tube: Waterloo. Map p 128.*

★★ St. James's Piccadilly

ST. JAMES   This gorgeous old Wren-designed church hosts 50-minute lunchtime classical recitals (Mon, Wed, and Fri at 1pm—a donation of £3 is suggested) and evening concerts as well. *197 Piccadilly.* ☎ *0207/381-0441. www.st-james-piccadilly.org. Tickets free–£20. Tube: Piccadilly. Map p 128.*

★★★ St. Martin-in-the-Fields

WEST END   Follow (allegedly) in Mozart's footsteps, and attend a concert at this atmospheric church. Admission to its popular lunchtime concerts (Mon, Tues, and Fri at 1pm) is by suggested donation (£3.50). The candlelit evening musicales are one of London's best deals. *Trafalgar Sq.* ☎ *0207/839-8362. www.stmartin-in-the-fields.org. Tickets £6–£18. Tube: Charing Cross. Map p 128.*

★★★ Wigmore Hall   MARYLEBONE

Bechstein Pianos built this grand Renaissance-style recital hall—one of the world's finest—in 1901. The greatest names in classical music

The Royal Opera House.

St. Martin-in-the-Fields.

have taken advantage of this venue's fabulous acoustics. *36 Wigmore St.* ☎ *0207/935-2141. www.wigmore-hall.org.uk. Tickets £9–£40. Tube: Bond St. Map p 128.*

Dance

★★ The Place   BLOOMSBURY

Dedicated to both the teaching and performing of dance, this small venue is *the* place in London to see contemporary new artists and startling modern dance. *17 Duke's Rd.* ☎ *0207/387-0013. www.theplace.org. Tickets £5–£20. Tube: Euston. Map p 128.*

★★★ Royal Opera House

COVENT GARDEN   The brilliantly restored 19th-century ROH houses the even more brilliant Royal Ballet, a company on a par with the world's best. You can catch any number of classics, such as *Giselle* or *Sleeping Beauty,* but you'll pay for the privilege. *Covent Garden.* ☎ *0207/304-4000. www.royaloperahouse.org. Tickets £5–£175. Tube: Covent Garden. Map p 128.*

★★★ Sadler's Wells   ISLINGTON

The best dance troupes in the world—from cutting-edge to classical—are delighted to perform at this chic theater, where they are assured of modern facilities and an appreciative audience. *Rosebery Ave.* ☎ *0207/863-8198. www.sadlers-wells.com. Tickets £8–£45. Tube: Angel. Map p 128.*

The Best Arts & Entertainment

Movies

★★ Chelsea Cinema CHELSEA

One of London's best art-house theaters, it may not have popcorn, but it does show intelligent films on a large screen (and the sound system is great, too). For a little more cash you can sit in large, well-placed "Pullman seats," with extra legroom—money well spent. *206 King's Rd.* ☎ *0207/351-3742. Tickets £7.50–£8.50. Tube: Sloane Sq. Map p 128.*

★★ Curzon Mayfair MAYFAIR

This historic art-house theater (it dates back to 1934) has been modernized and is famous for screening first-run films by Britain's famed Merchant-Ivory Productions. *38 Curzon St.* ☎ *0207/495-0500. www. curzoncinemas.com. Tickets £8.50. Tube: Green Park. Map p 128.*

★★★ kids The Electric Cinema

NOTTING HILL   Couches and leather seats, cocktails and yummy treats, Sunday double features, and a weekly

The Electric Cinema is one of London's best art-house theaters.

A statue at the Barbican Theatre, home of the Royal Shakespeare Company.

mom-and-baby screening make this art house a destination theater. Mainstream and independent films are shown. *191 Portobello Rd.* ☎ *0207/ 908-9696. www.the-electric.co.uk. Tickets £8–£13. Tube: Ladbroke Grove. Map p 128.*

★★★ Prince Charles SOHO   One

of London's best movie bargains, this independent theater offers sing-a-long sessions of *The Sound of Music*, cult hits, mainstream classics, and first-run foreign flicks. *7 Leicester Place.* ☎ *0901/272-7007. www. princecharlescinema.com. Tickets £1.50–£4. Tube: Leicester Sq. Map p 128.*

Theater

★★★ Barbican Theatre THE CITY

The London home of the Royal Shakespeare Company is one of the world's finest. Three productions are staged each week inside the 2,000-seat main auditorium, which offers excellent sightlines. *Silk St.* ☎ *020/7638-8891. www.barbican. org.uk. Tickets £5–£40. Tube: Barbican or Moorgate. Map p 128.*

★★★ **Old Vic Theatre** SOUTH-BANK   Except for a few war-time interruptions, this venerable theater has been in continuous operation since 1818. The repertory troupe at "the actors' theatre" has included a veritable Who's Who of thespians over the years, including Sir Laurence Olivier, Dame Maggie Smith, and the Redgrave clan. *The Cut, SE1.* 📞 *0870/060-6628. www.oldvic theatre.com. Tickets £15–£50. Tube: Waterloo. Map p 128.*

★★ **Open Air Theatre** MARYLE-BONE   The setting is idyllic, and the seating and acoustics are excellent at this Regent's Park venue. Presentations are mainly of Shakespeare's plays, usually in period costume. The season runs from June to mid-September. *Inner Circle, Regent's Park.* 📞 *0870/060-1811. http://openairtheatre.org. Tickets £8.50–£25. Tube: Baker St. Map p 128.*

★★ **Royal Court Theatre** CHELSEA   This leader in provocative, cutting-edge theater is home to the English Stage Company, which was formed to promote serious drama. *Sloane Sq.* 📞 *020/7565-5000. www. royalcourttheatre.com. Tickets £7.50–£28. Tube: Sloane Sq. Map p 128.*

★★★ **Royal National Theatre** SOUTHBANK   Home to one of the world's greatest stage companies, the Royal National presents the finest in world theater, from classic drama to award-winning new plays, comedies, and musicals. *South Bank.* 📞 *020/7452-3000. www.nt-online. org. Tickets £11–£40. Tube: Waterloo or Charing Cross. Map p 128.*

★★★ **Shakespeare's Globe Theatre** SOUTHBANK   This outdoor theater is a replica of the Elizabethan original, with wooden benches (you can rent a cushion) and thatched galleries. It's the perfect spot to watch the Bard's works. *New Globe Walk, Bankside.* 📞 *020/ 7902-1400. www.shakespeare-globe. org. Tickets £5 groundlings, £11–£29 gallery seats. Tube: Blackfriars. Map p 128.*

Buying **Theater Tickets**

You can buy advance tickets for most of London's entertainment venues through the theaters' websites or through **Ticketmaster** (www.ticketmaster.co.uk). Expect to pay a booking fee of £1 to £3 per ticket. Some concierges can set aside theater tickets for hotel guests, so ask when booking your room.

For same-day, half-price tickets, your best bet is the **TKTS booth** (www.officiallondontheatre.co.uk) in the Clock Tower on the south side of Leicester Square, which opens at noon. Two boards list the day's available West End shows. The blockbusters will probably be MIA, but decent seats at all the longer-running productions should be available. Many theaters sell their own half-price standby tickets at the box office about an hour before curtain time.

Last Minute (www.lastminute.com) has scads of good deals on theater-dinner packages, but read the fine print carefully—some may have restrictions and booking fees that add up to more than £10.

West End Theaters

1 Adelphi Theatre, Strand. ☎ 0207/344-0055

2 Albery Theatre, 85 St. Martin's Lane. ☎ 0207/438-9700

3 Aldwych Theatre, Aldwych. ☎ 0870/400-0650

4 Apollo Theatre, 39 Shaftesbury Ave. ☎ 0870/890-1101

5 The Arts Theatre, 6–7 Great Newport St. ☎ 0207/836-2132

6 Cambridge Theatre, Earlham St. ☎ 0207/494-5080

7 Criterion Theatre, Piccadilly Circus. ☎ 0207/413-1437

8 Dominion Theatre, 268–269 Tottenham Court Rd. ☎ 0870/607-7400

9 Donmar Warehouse, 41 Earlham St. ☎ 0870/060-6624

10 Duchess Theatre, Catherine St. ☎ 0207/494-5075

11 Duke of York Theatre, 104 St. Martin's Lane. ☎ 0207/836-4615

12 Fortune Theatre, Russell St. ☎ 0207/494-5075

13 Garrick Theatre, 2 Charing Cross Rd. ☎ 0207/494-5085

14 Gielgud Theatre, Shaftesbury Ave. ☎ 0207/494-5065

15 Her Majesty's Theatre, Haymarket. ☎ 0870/890-1106

16 Lyceum Theatre, 21 Wellington St. ☎ 0870/606-3441

17 Lyric Theatre, Shaftesbury Ave. ☎ 0207/494-5399

18 New London Theatre, Drury Lane. ☎ 0207/242-9802

19 Palace Theatre, 109–113 Shaftesbury Ave. ☎ 0207/434-0909

20 Palladium Theatre, 8 Argyll St. ☎ 0207/494-5020

21 Phoenix Theatre, 110 Charing Cross. ☎ 0207/369-1733

22 Piccadilly Theatre, Denman St. ☎ 0207/478-8800

23 Playhouse Theatre, Northumberland Ave. ☎ 0207/839-4292

24 Prince Edward Theatre, 30 Old Compton St. ☎ 0207/447-5400

25 Prince of Wales Theatre, Coventry St. ☎ 0207/839-5972

26 Queen's Theatre, Shaftesbury Ave. (at Cambridge Circus). ☎ 0207/494-5040

27 St. Martin's Theatre, West St. ☎ 0870/162-8787

28 Savoy Theatre, Savoy Court, Strand. ☎ 0207/836-8888

29 Shaftesbury Theatre, 210 Shaftesbury Ave. ☎ 0207/379-5399

30 Strand Theatre, Aldwych. ☎ 0207/836-4144

31 Theatre Royal Drury Lane, Drury Lane. ☎ 0207/494-5050

32 Vaudeville Theatre, 404 Strand. ☎ 0870/890-0511

33 Whitehall Theatre, 14 Whitehall. ☎ 0207/321-5400

34 Wyndham's Theatre, Charing Cross Rd. ☎ 0207/369-1736 ●

Hotel Best Bets

Best **Historic Hotel**
★★★ Hazlitt's 1718 $$$$ *6 Frith St., W1 (p 146)*

Best **Hotel for Victoriana**
★★★ The Gore $$$ *189 Queen's Gate, SW7 (p 146)*

Best **View of Hyde Park**
★★★ The Lanesborough Hotel $$$$$ *Hyde Park Corner, SW1 (p 147)*

Best **Luxury Hotel**
★★★ Claridges $$$$$ *8 Brook St., W1 (p 144)*

Most **Refined Atmosphere**
★★★ The Rookery $$$$ *Peter's Lane, Cowcross St., EC1 (p 148)*

Best **Hotel for Royal Watching**
★★★ Duke's Hotel $$$$ *35 St. James's Place, SW1 (p 145)*

Best **Base for Museum-Hopping**
★★ The Gainsborough $$ *7–11 Queensberry Place, SW7 (p 146)*

Best **Views of London**
★★ London Marriott County Hall $$$$ *County Hall, SE1 (p 147)*

Best **Chance to Get a Good Package Deal**
★★ The Rembrandt Hotel $$$ *11 Thurloe Place, SW7 (p 148)*

Best **Hotel for Afternoon Tea**
★★★ The Basil Street Hotel $$$$ *Basil St., SW3 (p 144)*

Best **Value**
★★ Mowbray Court Hotel $ *28–32 Penywern St., SW5 (p 148)*

Best **Boutique Hotel**
★★★ The Franklin Hotel $$$ *28 Egerton Gardens, SW3 (p 146)*

A marble bathroom at the Dorchester.

Best **B&B**
★★ The Claverley $$ *13–14 Beaufort Gardens, SW3 (p 145)*

Best **Family Hotel**
★★ Lord Jim Hotel $ *23–25 Penywern St., SW5 (p 147)*

Most **Romantic Hotel**
★★★ Blakes $$$$$ *33 Roland Gardens, SW7 (p 144)*

Most **Quirky Decor**
★★★ Miller's Residence $$$ *111a Westbourne Grove, W2 (p 147)*

Best **Bathrooms**
★★★ The Dorchester $$$$$ *53 Park Lane, W1 (p 145)*

Best **Business Hotel**
★★ The Great Eastern Hotel $$$$$ *Liverpool St., EC2 (p 146)*

Best for **Theater Buffs**
★★ Thistle Piccadilly $$$$ *Coventry St., W1 (p 150)*

Best for **Shopaholics**
★★ The Cadogan Hotel $$$$ *5 Sloane St., SW1 (p 144)*

East End Hotels

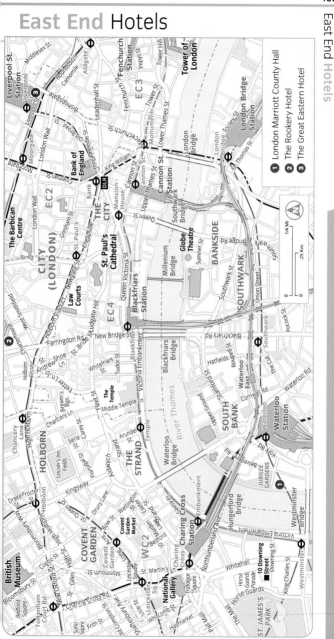

1 London Marriott County Hall
2 The Rookery Hotel
3 The Great Eastern Hotel

Chelsea Hotels

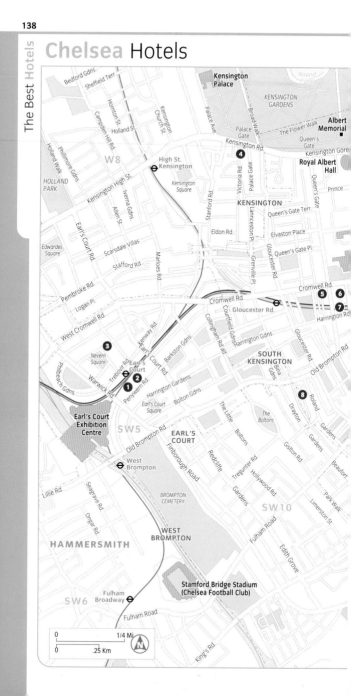

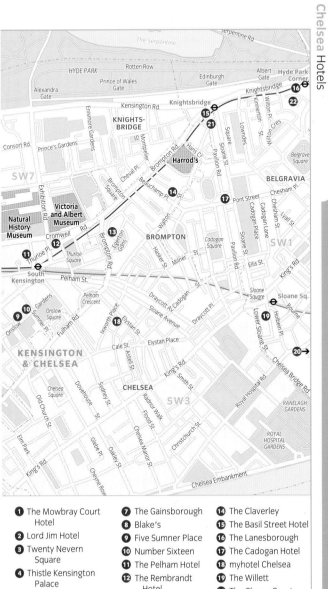

1 The Mowbray Court Hotel
2 Lord Jim Hotel
3 Twenty Nevern Square
4 Thistle Kensington Palace
5 The Gore
6 The Gallery Hotel
7 The Gainsborough
8 Blake's
9 Five Sumner Place
10 Number Sixteen
11 The Pelham Hotel
12 The Rembrandt Hotel
13 The Franklin Hotel
14 The Claverley
15 The Basil Street Hotel
16 The Lanesborough
17 The Cadogan Hotel
18 myhotel Chelsea
19 The Willett
20 The Cherry Court Hotel

Notting Hill Hotels

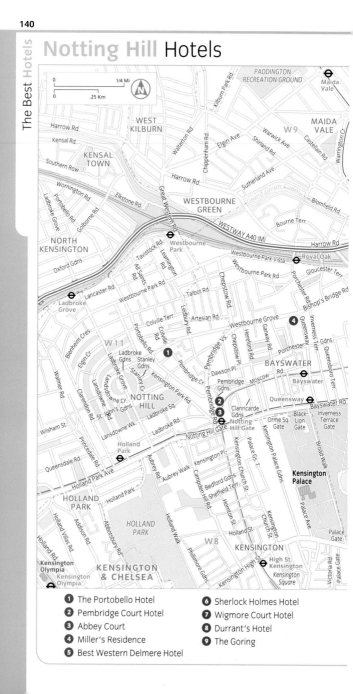

1. The Portobello Hotel
2. Pembridge Court Hotel
3. Abbey Court
4. Miller's Residence
5. Best Western Delmere Hotel
6. Sherlock Holmes Hotel
7. Wigmore Court Hotel
8. Durrant's Hotel
9. The Goring

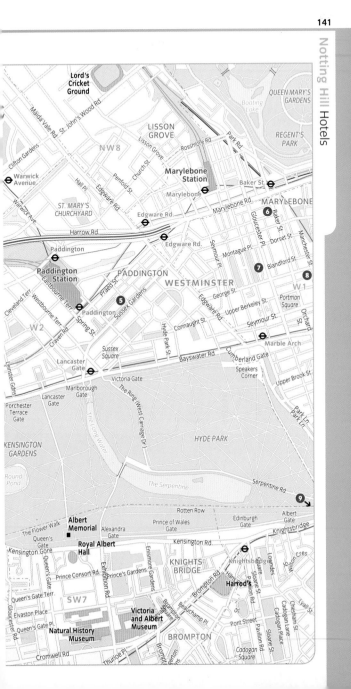

West End Hotels

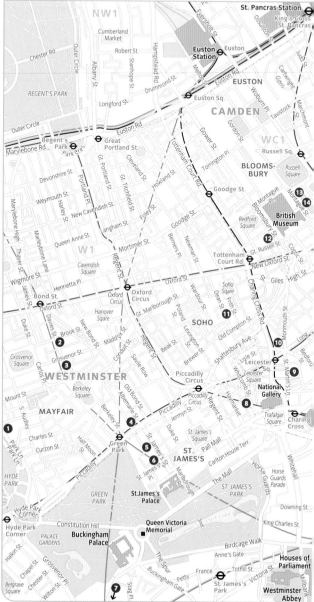

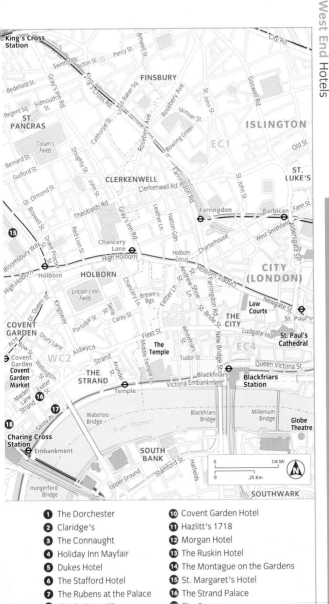

1. The Dorchester
2. Claridge's
3. The Connaught
4. Holiday Inn Mayfair
5. Dukes Hotel
6. The Stafford Hotel
7. The Rubens at the Palace
8. Thistle Piccadilly
9. St. Martins Lane
10. Covent Garden Hotel
11. Hazlitt's 1718
12. Morgan Hotel
13. The Ruskin Hotel
14. The Montague on the Gardens
15. St. Margaret's Hotel
16. The Strand Palace
17. The Savoy
18. The Adelphi Hotel

Hotels A to Z

★★ **kids** **Abbey Court** NOTTING HILL   This four-floor Victorian town house has considerable charms, if you can get along without an elevator. *20 Pembridge Gardens, W4.* ☎ *0207/221-7518. www.abbey courthotel.co.uk. 22 units. Doubles £150–£180 w/breakfast. AE, DC, MC, V. Tube: Notting Hill Gate. Map p 140.*

★ **kids** **The Adelphi Hotel** WEST END   It's a bit like a college dorm, with small, spartan rooms and no elevator, but what it lacks in charm it makes up for in value. *21 Villiers St., WC2.* ☎ *0207/930-8764. www. royaladelphi.co.uk. 47 units. Doubles £68–£90 w/breakfast. AE, DC, MC, V. Tube: Embankment. Map p 142.*

★★★ **kids** **The Basil Street Hotel** KNIGHTSBRIDGE   This charming, *veddy* English hotel is loaded with antiques, has a great location, and offers excellent afternoon tea. *Basil St., SW3.* ☎ *800/448-8355 in the U.S.; 0207/581-3311. www.the basil.com. 93 units. Doubles £205. AE, DC, MC, V. Tube: Knightsbridge. Map p 138.*

★★ **kids** **Best Western Delmere Hotel** PADDINGTON Housed in an enlarged Victorian town house, this property is centrally located, has a reasonably attractive decor, and offers good package deals. *130 Sussex Gardens, W2.* ☎ *0207/706-3344. www.bw-del merehotel.co.uk. 36 units. Doubles £112–£121 w/breakfast. AE, DC, MC, V. Tube: Paddington. Map p 140.*

★★★ **Blakes** SOUTH KENSINGTON Many of the U.K.'s young celebs flock to this trendy hotel, noted for its exotic and lavish decor. It serves the best homemade scones in town. *33 Roland Gardens, SW7.* ☎ *0207/ 370-6701. www.blakeshotels.com.*

The Corfu Suite at Blakes hotel.

47 units. Doubles £275–£345. AE, DC, MC, V. Tube: Gloucester Rd. Map p 138.

★★ **kids** **The Cadogan Hotel** CHELSEA   Famous as the spot where Oscar Wilde was arrested, this terribly civilized hotel is a great place for shoppers to hide out. *5 Sloane St., SW1.* ☎ *0207/235-7141. www. cadogan.com. 65 units. Doubles £245–£300. AE, DC, MC, V. Tube: Knightsbridge or Sloane Sq. Map p 138.*

★ **kids** **The Cherry Court Hotel** PIMLICO   They don't come much cheaper than this pleasant hotel, at least not with the same degree of cleanliness and comfort. *23 Hugh St., SW1.* ☎ *0207/828-2840. www. cherrycourthotel.co.uk. 12 units. Doubles £60–£120 w/breakfast. Add 5% for credit cards. AE, MC, V. Tube: Victoria. Map p 138.*

★★★ **kids** **Claridge's** MAYFAIR This redoubtable London institution, close to Bond Street's shopping, has been the final word in elegance for decades. Rooms are spacious and service is impeccable. *Brook St., W1.* ☎ *0207/629-8860. www.savoy-group.*

com. 203 units. Doubles £395–£420. AE, DC, MC, V. Tube: Bond St. Map p 142.

★★ **kids** **The Claverley** KNIGHTSBRIDGE A very popular, award-winning B&B around the corner from Harrods and within walking distance of Hyde Park. 13–14 Beaufort Gardens, SW3. ☎ 800/747-0398 in the U.S.; 0207/589-8541. www.claverleyhotel. fsnet.co.uk. 33 units. Doubles £135–£195 w/breakfast. AE, DC, MC, V. Tube: Knightsbridge. Map p 138.

★★★ **The Connaught** MAYFAIR With all the stately grandeur of an old-style gentlemen's club, the Connaught is as dignified as the neighborhood around it. Very atmospheric. 16 Carlos Place, W1. ☎ 0207/499-7070. www.savoy-group.com. 92 units. Doubles £250 and up. AE, DC, MC, V. Tube: Bond St. Map p 142.

★★★ **kids** **Covent Garden Hotel** SOHO Big beds, relatively large rooms, and a deft English decor make this popular hotel one of the best in Soho. The neighborhood gets a bit rowdy at night and touristy during the day. 10 Monmouth St., WC2. ☎ 0207/806-1000. www.firmdale. com. 50 units. Doubles £210–£285.

AE, DC, MC, V. Tube: Covent Garden. Map p 142.

★★★ **The Dorchester** MAYFAIR This opulent gem welcomes kings and commoners with equal panache. Elegant decor, first-rate amenities, and to-die-for bathrooms. 53 Park Lane, W1. ☎ 800/727-9820 in the U.S.; 0207/629-8888. www.dorchesterhotel. com. 248 units. Doubles £330–£385. AE, DC, MC, V. Tube: Hyde Park Corner. Map p 142.

★★★ **Dukes Hotel** ST. JAMES'S Very intimate and genteel, from the gas-lit courtyard and spiffy rooms, to the penthouse suite with views over London. Elegant, but not snotty. 35 St. James's Place, SW1. ☎ 800/381-4702 in the U.S.; 0207/491-4840. www.dukeshotel.co.uk. 89 units. Doubles £235–£280. AE, DC, MC, V. Tube: Green Park. Map p 142.

★★ **kids** **Durrant's Hotel** MARYLEBONE This clubby hotel offers good value and a great location close to Oxford Street's shopping and the Wallace Collection. George St., W1. ☎ 0207/935-8131. www.durrantshotel.co.uk. 92 units. Doubles £165–£250. AE, MC, V. Tube: Bond St. Map p 140.

A London institution, Claridge's is renowned for its elegant public rooms.

★★★ Five Sumner Place

SOUTH KENSINGTON   One of London's best small, no-frills hotels, the Sumner is well-loved by clued-in visitors, so book way ahead. *5 Sumner Place, SW7. ☎ 0207/584-7586. www.sumnerplace.com. 13 units. Doubles £130–£150 w/breakfast. AE, DC, MC, V. Tube: S. Kensington. Map p 138.*

★★★ kids The Franklin Hotel

KNIGHTSBRIDGE   Convenient, quiet, and refined, many rooms overlook a garden. *28 Egerton Gardens, SW3. ☎ 0207/584-5533. www.franklin hotel.co.uk. 47 units. Doubles £190–£325. AE, DC, MC, V. Tube: Knightsbridge. Map p 138.*

★★ kids The Gainsborough

SOUTH KENSINGTON   A stone's throw from the Natural History Museum, this hotel offers well-appointed rooms at a decent price. *7–11 Queensberry Place, SW7. ☎ 800/270-9206 in the U.S.; 0207/838-1700. www.eeh.co.uk. 49 units. Doubles £88–£150 w/breakfast. AE, DC, MC, V. Tube: S. Kensington. Map p 138.*

An elegant four-poster suite at The Gainsborough in South Kensington.

★★ kids The Gallery Hotel

SOUTH KENSINGTON   This Victorian hotel's pluses include small but comfortable rooms with attractive marble bathrooms, and a great breakfast. *8–10 Queensbury Place, SW7. ☎ 800/270-9206 in the U.S.; 0207/970-1805. www.eeh.co.uk. 37 units. Doubles £140–£160 w/breakfast. AE, DC, MC, V. Tube: S. Kensington. Map p 138.*

★★★ kids The Gore SOUTH

KENSINGTON   Every room inside this gorgeous re-creation of an early Victorian hotel is individually decorated with fine antiques. *189 Queen's Gate, SW7. ☎ 0207/584-6601. www.gorehotel.co.uk. 48 units. Doubles £150–£170. AE, DC, MC, V. Tube: Gloucester Rd. Map p 138.*

★★★ kids The Goring PIMLICO

A stone's throw from Victoria Station, this hotel has the feel of a country house, with a big walled garden and a charming lobby. *Beeston Place, SW1. ☎ 0207/396-9000. www.goringhotel.co.uk. 75 units. Doubles £255–£395. AE, DC, MC, V. Tube: Victoria. Map p 140.*

★★ kids The Great Eastern Hotel EAST END   This former

Victorian train-station hotel now offers the best business digs in The City. *Liverpool St., EC2. ☎ 0207/618-5000. www.great-eastern-hotel.co.uk. 267 units. Doubles £285–£305. AE, DC, MC, V. Tube: Liverpool St. Map p 137.*

★★★ Hazlitt's 1718 SOHO

Favored by the literary set, the 18th-century-flavored Hazlitt's feels more like a boarding house than a hotel. There's no elevator. *6 Frith St., W1. ☎ 0207/434-1771. www.hazlittshotel.com. 23 units. Doubles £205–£255. AE, DC, MC, V. Tube: Tottenham Court. Map p 142.*

★★ kids Holiday Inn Mayfair

MAYFAIR   The rack rates at this plain-Jane hotel are high, but you

The antiques-filled lounge at trendy Miller's Residence in Notting Hill.

can get a bargain on the Internet, making it a good bet in deluxe Mayfair. *3 Berkeley St., W1.* ☎ *0870/400-9110. www.mayfair.holiday-inn.com. 184 units. Doubles £180–£255. AE, DC, MC, V. Tube: Green Park. Map p 142.*

★★★ **kids** **The Lanesborough** KNIGHTSBRIDGE   Housed in a former hospital building, this ultraluxe Regency-style hotel features state-of-the-art amenities—and your very own butler. *Hyde Park Corner, SW1.* ☎ *0207/259-5599. www.lanesborough. com. 95 units. Doubles £395–£475. AE, DC, MC, V. Tube: Hyde Park Corner. Map p 138.*

★★ **kids** **London Marriott County Hall** SOUTH BANK   You can't beat the views of Big Ben and Parliament from this historic hotel's rooms, though the prices are steep. *County Hall, SE1.* ☎ *888/236-2427 in the U.S.; 0207/928-5200. www. marriotthotels.com. 186 units. Doubles £239–£400. AE, DC, MC, V. Tube: Waterloo. Map p 137.*

★★ **kids** **Lord Jim Hotel** EARL'S COURT   Known for its attractive package deals, this budget hotel offers plainly but pleasantly decorated rooms; families will fit easily inside the bigger rooms. *23–25 Penywern St., SW5.* ☎ *0207/370-6071.*

www.lgh-hotels.com. 50 units. Doubles £65–£90 w/breakfast. AE, DC, MC, V. Tube: Earl's Court. Map p 138.

★★★ **kids** **Miller's Residence** NOTTING HILL   Brimming with antiques, this well-regarded hotel sports a wild, rococo decor and a trendy neighborhood location. *111a Westbourne Grove, W2.* ☎ *0207/243-1024. www.millersuk. com. 8 units. Doubles £150–£185 w/breakfast. AE, MC, V. Tube: Bayswater. Map p 140.*

★★ **kids** **The Montague on the Gardens** BLOOMSBURY   In the shadow of the British Museum, this deluxe, country-style hotel features a garden and a ton of amenities. *15 Montague St.* ☎ *800/424-2862 in the U.S.; 0207/637-1001. www. montaguehotel.com. 105 units. Doubles £220–£350. AE, DC, MC, V. Tube: Russell Sq. Map p 142.*

★★ **kids** **Morgan Hotel** BLOOMS-BURY   The family-run Morgan features well-kept Georgian-style rooms. It's an old favorite of Anglophiles who can't get enough of the nearby British Museum. *24 Bloomsbury St., WC1.* ☎ *0207/ 636-3735. 21 units. Doubles £98– £130 w/breakfast. MC, V. Tube: Tottenham Court. Map p 142.*

★★ kids The Mowbray Court Hotel

EARL'S COURT This spotless budget hotel, run by a friendly Irish family, features basic rooms, some without private bathrooms. *28–32 Penywern Rd., SW5.* ☎ *0207/370-2316. www.mowbraycourthotel.co.uk. 80 units. Doubles £67–£80 w/breakfast. AE, DC, MC, V. Tube: Earl's Court. Map p 138.*

★★ kids myhotel Chelsea

CHELSEA This Asian-flavored boutique hotel is understated but luxurious, offering a wide range of amenities. Very quiet and peaceful. *35 Ixworth Place, SW3.* ☎ *0207/225-7500. www.myhotels.co.uk. 45 units. Doubles £150–£250. AE, DC, MC, V. Tube: S. Kensington. Map p 138.*

★★★ kids Number Sixteen

SOUTH KENSINGTON This modernized Victorian town-house hotel is popular with Americans, quiet, and reasonably priced. *16 Sumner Place, SW7.* ☎ *0207/589-5232. www.numbersixteenhotel.co.uk. 42 units. Doubles £150–£240. AE, DC, MC, V. Tube: S. Kensington. Map p 138.*

★★★ kids The Pelham Hotel

SOUTH KENSINGTON The centrally located Pelham has a friendly staff and accommodations exquisitely decorated in an English country style. Beware the noisy front rooms. *15 Cromwell Place, SW7.* ☎ *0207/589-8288. www.firmdalehotels.com. 46 units. Doubles £160–£250. AE, DC, MC, V. Tube: S. Kensington. Map p 138.*

★★★ kids Pembridge Court Hotel

NOTTING HILL This well-kept Victorian town house has a beautiful decor; the homey atmosphere is accentuated by the resident cat. *34 Pembridge Gardens, W11.* ☎ *800/709-9882 in the U.S.; 0207/229-9977. www.pemct.co.uk. 20 units. Doubles £160–£195 w/breakfast. AE, DC, MC, V. Tube: Notting Hill Gate. Map p 140.*

★★★ The Portobello Hotel

NOTTING HILL Sumptuously decorated guest rooms mark this trendy hotel—a hit with the music and modeling set—located near Portobello Road. *22 Stanley Gardens, W1.* ☎ *0207/727-2777. www.portobello-hotel.co.uk. 24 units. Doubles £160–£275 w/breakfast. AE, DC, MC, V. Tube: Notting Hill Gate. Map p 140.*

★★ kids The Rembrandt Hotel

SOUTH KENSINGTON This solid tourist hotel across from the V&A is popular with groups and offers clean but bland rooms. *11 Thurloe Place, SW7.* ☎ *0207/589-8100. www.sarova.co.uk. 195 units. Doubles £215–£240 w/breakfast. AE, DC, MC, V. Tube: S. Kensington. Map p 138.*

★★★ The Rookery Hotel

EAST END This sure-footed evocation of a bygone era is set on the edge of The City; each room is individually decorated with rare antiques.

Notting Hill's Pembridge Court Hotel features a homey atmosphere.

Peter's Lane, Cowcross St., EC1.
☎ 0207/336-0931. www.rookery
hotel.com. 33 units. Doubles
£225–£275. AE, DC, MC, V. Tube:
Farringdon. Map p 137.

★★ The Rubens at the Palace

VICTORIA   Traditional English hos-
pitality is combined with the latest
in creature comforts. The Royal
Rooms have the most atmosphere.
39 Buckingham Palace Rd., SW1.
☎ 877/955-1515 in the U.S.; 0207/
834-6600. www.rubenshotel.com.
172 units. Doubles £210–£480. AE,
DC, MC, V. Tube: Victoria. Map p 142.

★ kids The Ruskin Hotel

BLOOMSBURY   The clean, friendly,
no-frills B&B in an old town house
is located opposite the British
Museum. There's an elevator. 23–24
Montague St., WC1. ☎ 0207/636-
7388. www.ruskinhotellondon.com.
33 units. Doubles £84–£88 w/break-
fast. AE, DC, MC, V. Tube: Russell Sq.
Map p 142.

★ kids St. Margaret's Hotel

BLOOMSBURY   This economical
hotel feels like a really nice hostel
with private rooms, but you don't
have to clear out for the day. Relax
in the garden. 26 Bedford Place,
WC1. ☎ 0207/636-4277. www.st
margaretshotel.co.uk. 64 units. Doubles £92–£99 w/breakfast. AE, DC,
MC, V. Tube: Russell Sq. Map p 142.

★★ St. Martin's Lane SOHO

Hotelier Ian Schrager's minimalist
shrine to New York chic is modern,
but the service can be shabby, and
the rooms tiny and expensive. 45 St.
Martin's Lane, WC2. ☎ 0207/300-
5500. www.morganshotelgroup.com.
204 units. Doubles £225–£270. AE,
DC, MC, V. Tube: Leicester Sq. Map
p 142.

★★★ kids The Savoy COVENT

GARDEN   This grande dame contin-
ues to improve on its old-world elegance and is the gold standard for

The George I room, one of the Royal
Rooms at the Rubens at the Palace.

London's swanky hotels. 1 Savoy
Hill. ☎ 800/637-2869 in the U.S.;
0207/950-5492. www.savoy-group-co.
uk. 161 units. Doubles £400–£700.
AE, DC, MC, V. Tube: Charing Cross.
Map p 142.

★★ kids Sherlock Holmes

Hotel MARYLEBONE   This modern
boutique hotel with large rooms is
close to Regent's Park and Oxford
Street but hardly Sherlockian in
decor. 108 Baker St., W1. ☎ 0207/
486-6161. www.sherlockholmes
hotel.com. 119 units. Doubles
£215–£260. AE, DC, MC, V. Tube:
Baker St. Map p 140.

★★★ kids The Stafford Hotel

MAYFAIR/ST. JAMES   This gorgeous
18th-century hotel, set in a grand
old neighborhood, combines
English country style with modern
amenities. St. James's Place, SW1.
☎ 0207/493-0111. www.thestafford
hotel.co.uk. 81 units. Doubles £250–
£335. AE, DC, MC, V. Tube: Green
Park. Map p 142.

A deluxe double at The Willet, a classic Victorian boutique hotel.

★★ **kids** **The Strand Palace**
COVENT GARDEN This big old hotel is more utilitarian than deluxe in decor, but nevertheless offers solid quality and service. Ask for upgrades and special deals. *372 Strand, WC2.* ☎ *0207/379-4737. www.strand palace.co.uk. 783 units. Doubles £170–£200 w/breakfast. AE, DC, MC, V. Tube: Embankment. Map p 142.*

★★ **kids** **Thistle Kensington Palace** SOUTH KENSINGTON
Check in here for pleasant rooms, good deals year-round, and a location close to Kensington Palace. *DeVere Gardens.* ☎ *0870/333-9111. www.thistlehotels.com/kensington palace. 285 units. Doubles £120–£188 w/breakfast. AE, DC, MC, V. Tube: Gloucester Rd. Map p 138.*

★★ **kids** **Thistle Piccadilly** PICCADILLY There's no better location for those who want to hit the theaters and shops of the West End. Check the website for packages and promotions. *Coventry St., W1.* ☎ *0870/333-9118. www.thistle hotels.com. 92 units. Doubles £220–£288 w/breakfast. AE, DC, MC, V. Tube: Piccadilly. Map p 142.*

★★ **Twenty Nevern Square**
EARLS COURT An elegant European-Asian decor, a full range of amenities, and a garden make this one of the more sumptuous B&Bs in London. *20 Nevern Sq., SW5.* ☎ *0207/565-9555. www.twenty nevernsquare.co.uk. 20 units. Doubles £175–£195 w/breakfast. AE, DC, MC, V. Tube: Earls Court. Map p 138.*

★ **kids** **Wigmore Court Hotel**
MARYLEBONE Clean, friendly, and well located, the Wigmore Court is a favorite of the budget-conscious and is well-suited to family groups. *23 Gloucester Place, W1.* ☎ *0207/ 935-0928. www.wigmore-court-hotel. co.uk. 16 units. Doubles £89–£98 w/breakfast. MC, V. Tube: Marble Arch. Map p 140.*

★★ **kids** **The Willett** CHELSEA
This charming and reasonably priced boutique hotel features a lovely Victorian decor and an elegant breakfast room. Some standard rooms are tiny. *32 Sloane Gardens, SW3.* ☎ *0207/824-8415. www.eeh.co.uk. 36 units. Doubles £105–£160 w/breakfast. AE, DC, MC, V. Tube: Sloane Sq. Map p 138.* ●

The
Savvy Traveler

Before You Go

Government Tourist Offices

IN THE U.S.: Visit Britain, 551 Fifth Ave., 7th floor, New York, NY 10176 (☎ 800/462-2748). **IN CANADA:** Visit Britain, 5915 Airport Rd., Suite 120, Mississauga, Ontario L4V 1T1 (☎ 905/405-1840). **IN IRELAND:** Visit Britain, 18–19 College Green, Dublin 2 (☎ 01/670-8000). **IN AUSTRALIA:** Visit Britain, level 16, Gateway, 1 Macquarie Place, Sydney, NSW 2000 (☎ 029/377-4400). **IN NEW ZEALAND:** Visit Britain, Fay Rich White Building, 151 Queen St., Auckland 1 (☎ 09/303-1446). The best place for information, regardless of your home country, is on the Web at www.visit britain.com.

The Best Time to Go

Though prices are highest in spring and summer, the weather is best then, with only occasional showers. Sunny and warm August is a sensible time to visit because many Londoners go on vacation, hotel rates drop, and London's notorious traffic lightens up. The only problem is all those tourists, looking for a genuine British experience, and a reduction in services (closed restaurants, and the like). Fares are cheapest between November and March. The city's museum and theater scenes are in full swing in winter, but the city can get dark and chilly and bleak. September and early October can be gray and rainy, too, but most gardens are still in bloom.

Festivals and Special Events

For more information on London events, check out the following websites: *www.visitlondon.com; www.londontown.com; www.thisis london.com; www.timeout.com; and www.golondon.co.uk.*

JAN. The full-dress **Charles I Commemoration** that marks the king's beheading is held on the last Sunday of the month. A must-see for history buffs. ☎ *0207/930-4179, www.hrp.org.uk.*

FEB. **Chinese New Year** is celebrated in Soho's Chinatown with the requisite dancing lions and red confetti. *www.chinatown-online.co.uk.* **The Great Spitalfields Pancake Race** on Shrove Tuesday (called Pancake Day in London) is a bizarre old tradition that combines tossed pancakes and teams of runners. ☎ *0207/375-0441.*

MAR. The month's best-loved events are boat races: the **Head of the River Race** from Mortlake to Putney Bridge, *www.horr.co.uk*; and the **Oxford & Cambridge Boat Race** in the opposite direction. *www.the boatrace.org*. There are a number of good pubs and vantage points along the 6.5km (4-mile) stretch, but Hammersmith and Putney bridges are the best places to watch.

APR. More than 30,000 people run the **London Marathon** every year; The 42km (26-mile) course runs from Greenwich Park to St. James's Park. The best views are from Victoria Embankment. *www.london marathon.co.uk.*

MAY. A difficult ticket, the **Chelsea Flower Show** is a wonderful spectacle, with very creative garden displays. ☎ *0207/649 1885, www.rhs. org.uk.*

JUNE. The **Royal Academy Summer Exhibition,** the world's largest, displays the works of artists of every genre and caliber. *www.royalacademy.org.uk*. **The Queen's Official Birthday** (Elizabeth II was actually born in Apr) is honored with a carriage ride, a gun salute, and the **Trooping of the Colours** at Horse Guards Parade. On **London Gardens Squares Day,** a number of gardens available only to private key-holders are open to an envious public. **Royal Ascot** is the big social horse event of the year, a time when the upper classes dust off their chapeaux and take part in the old tradition of betting on horses while dressed to the nines. *www.ascot.co.uk.* The **Lawn Tennis Championships at Wimbledon** need no introduction, but you will need a very-hard-to-get ticket (see "Spectator Sports," below). ☎ *0208/944-1066, www.wimbledon.org.*

JULY. **The Proms,** formally known as the BBC Sir Henry Wood Promenade Concerts, held in and outside Royal Albert Hall, are the annual joy of London's classical music lovers. ☎ *0207/589-8212, www.bbc.co.uk/proms.*

AUG. The **Notting Hill Festival,** one of the largest street festivals in Europe, is held in and around Portobello Road. Expect crowds, beer, and spicy Caribbean cuisine. *www.portowebbo.co.uk.*

SEPT. During the 2-day **Open House,** hundreds of usually inaccessible architectural gems are opened to the public. *www.londonopenhouse.org.* Several hundred boats of every description ply the Thames from Richmond to Greenwich in the **Great River Race,** which is less a race than a proud parade of maritime multiculturalism. *www.greatriverrace.co.uk.*

OCT. At the 125-year-old **Pearly Kings & Queens Harvest Festival,** the descendants of London's cockney Costermongers (market traders) dress in costumes covered with pearly buttons and gather at a church service at St. Martin-in-the-Fields for charity—and to show off their button-sewing prowess. ☎ *0207/766 1100, www.pearly society.co.uk.* Floats and carriages make their way from Mansion House to the Royal Courts of Justice and back again during **The Lord Mayor's Show.** *www.lordmayorsshow.org.*

NOV. **Guy Fawkes Night** commemorates the thwarted destruction of Parliament with bonfires and fireworks all over London. Book a couple of spins on the London Eye (p 12, bullet 7) after dark so you can see London's sky lit up from near and far.

DEC. For the horse-mad, there is no better fun than the **International Show-jumping Championships** in Kensington. ☎ *0207/370-8202, www.olympiashowjumping.com.*

The Weather

London's notorious (man-made) pea-soup fogs have long been eradicated, but a tendency toward showers and gray skies is ever-present—particularly November through March, when the sun shows its face only briefly. The weather can be fickle, and experiencing all four seasons in the span of a single day is not an unlikely possibility. (If staying dry matters to you, don't arrive without an umbrella!) The general climate is relatively mild, never going much above 75°F (23°C) or below 40°F (5°C). There are no great extremes, except for a few unpleasant dog days in summer (when a temp of 80°F/27°C is considered a heat wave) and the rare freezing snowfall during the short, dark days of a bleak mid-winter.

What to Pack

It's best to dress in layers in order to be prepared for a range of temperatures in a single day, no matter what the season. If you plan on dining in some of the city's nicer restaurants, pack a jacket or dress and shoes. Most visitors will never regret bringing a raincoat and a collapsible umbrella. Comfortable walking shoes are a must. A warm sweater

LONDON'S AVERAGE TEMPERATURE & RAINFALL

	JAN	FEB	MAR	APR	MAY	JUNE
Daily Temp (°F)	43	44	50	55	63	68
Daily Temp (°C)	6	7	10	13	17	20
Avg. Rainfall (in/mm)	3/54	1.5/40	1.5/37	1.5/37	1.8/46	1.8/45

	JULY	AUG	SEPT	OCT	NOV	DEC
Daily Temp (°F)	72	70	66	57	50	44
Daily Temp (°C)	22	21	19	14	10	7
Avg. Rainfall (in/mm)	2.2/57	2.3/59	1.9/49	2.2/57	2.5/64	1.9/48

and gloves in the winter, and a hot-weather ensemble in summer, will come in handy.

Other items to include:

- Any medications you need. Ask your doctor for backup prescriptions (London pharmacies will fill them) just in case you lose your meds.
- A backup pair of eyeglasses.
- Toiletries and film (both are very expensive in London).
- A copy of your passport's information page and all vital documents in case of loss or theft.
- An electrical adapter and/or converter if you plan on bringing any electrical appliances such as digital camera rechargers. (Don't bring hair dryers, which require a cumbersome converter/transformer—most London hotels provide them.) Laptops usually have their own built-in electrical converter, but you'll need a plug adaptor for the U.K.'s three-prong plugs.

Useful Websites

- **www.visitbritain.com:** Great Britain's official tourist website features lots of useful information and trip-planning advice.
- **www.londontown.com:** The official London Tourist Board site offers specials on hotels, sells theater tickets, and has lots of useful information.
- **www.visitlondon.com:** London's official website features loads of information and lets you book hotels, buy discount passes, and more.
- **www.thisislondon.co.uk:** The *Evening Standard*'s website is a good source of current entertainment and restaurant information.
- **www.timeout.com:** The weekly magazine features cultural event listings, as well as information on entertainment, restaurants, and nightlife.
- **www.londontransport.co.uk:** Your best source of information on London's public transportation system, including the Tube, buses, and ferries.
- **www.royal.gov.uk:** If you're a royal watcher, or are just looking for information, trivia, or anything else about the British royal family, direct your browser to this site.
- **www.streetmap.co.uk:** This site offers detailed London street maps and directions to specific addresses.

How to Get the Best Airfare

Besides traveling during the off season, when you can usually get cheap fares and promotional specials directly from the airlines, try the following:

- **Book on the Web.** The "Big Three" online travel agencies—Expedia.com, Orbitz, and Travelocity—often feature discounted fares. Another good website for low airfares to London is www.cheaptickets.com. Note also that booking your ticket on the major airlines' websites will usually save you cash.

- **Use a Consolidator.** Also known as a bucket shop, these agencies usually offer good international fare deals. Reputable consolidators include **FLIGHTS.COM** (☎ 201/541-3867; www.flights.com); **STA TRAVEL** (www. Statravel.co. uk), which caters to students and those under 26; and **FLY-CHEAP** (☎ 800/359-2432; www. flycheap.com).

- **Bid on a Flight.** If you're willing to give up some control over your flight details, use an opaque fare service such as **PRICELINE** (www.priceline.com; www. priceline.co.uk for Europeans) or **HOTWIRE** (www.hotwire.com). Both offer rock-bottom prices in exchange for travel on a "mystery airline" at a mysterious time of day. The mystery airlines are all major, well-known carriers, but your chances of getting an odd flight time or having to change planes are good.

Cellphones

The three letters that define much of the world's wireless capabilities are GSM (Global System for Mobiles), a big, seamless network that makes for easy cross-border cellphone use throughout Europe and dozens of other countries worldwide. You can make and receive calls in London, though you will accrue whopping roaming charges.

International visitors can buy a pay-as-you-go mobile phone at any phone store in London. This gives you a local number and minutes that can be topped up with phone cards that can be purchased at newsagents. O2 and Vodaphone are the best service networks.

Your hotel may be able to rent you a cellphone while in London, though it won't be cheap; inquire before you arrive. North Americans can rent one before leaving home from **INTOUCH USA** (☎ 800/872-7626; www.intouchglobal.com) or **ROADPOST** (☎ 888/290-1606 or 905/272-5665; www.roadpost.com).

Car Rentals

In a word—don't. Driving in London is a royal pain and I strongly recommend against it. You're far better off sticking to public transportation when you take into account the congestion fee (a charge of £5 for entering an arbitrarily drawn central area of the city 7am–6:30pm), the dreadful traffic, the dearth of street parking, and (particularly for North Americans) the high price of petrol. If you still want to rent a vehicle, all major car rental companies operate in the U.K., and cars can be picked up at any of the major airports.

Getting **There**

By Plane

American, Air Canada, British Airways, Continental, Delta, Northwest, United, and Virgin Atlantic Airways offer nonstop service from various locations in the U.S. and Canada to London's major airports. **QANTAS** offers daily service to London from Sydney and Melbourne.

London is served by four airports. **LONDON HEATHROW AIRPORT** (☎ **0870/000-0123** for flight information), located 24km (15 miles) west of London, offers the quickest access to the city. The fastest way into town is the **HEATHROW EXPRESS** (☎ **0845/600-1515** or 877/677-1066; www.heathrowexpress.com) train to Paddington Station (15 min.; £13). You can also take a cheaper ride on the Underground's Piccadilly Line into Central London (40 min.; £6). Black cabs cost roughly £50 to center city.

Increasingly popular **GATWICK AIRPORT** (☎ **0870/002-468** for flight information) is 40km (25 miles) south of London. The fastest (and best) way to get to the city is via the **GATWICK EXPRESS** (☎ **0845/850-1530**; www.gatwickexpress.co.uk) trains to Victoria Station (30 min.; £11). A taxi ride into London usually takes an hour, and can cost up to £105.

STANSTED (☎ **0870/000-0303**) and **LUTON** (☎ **0158/240-5100**) airports handle mostly short-hop flights on bargain airlines (usually easyJet and Ryanair) from European and U.K. destinations. Both are more than 80km (50 miles) from London. To get from Stansted to the city, take a **STANSTED EXPRESS** (☎ **0845/850-0150**; www.stanstedexpress.com) train to Liverpool Street Station (45 min.; £15). From Luton, take **GREENLINE BUS NO.**

757 (☎ **0870/608-2608**) to Victoria Station (1 hr. 39 min.; £13).

By Train

The **EUROSTAR** provides direct train service between Paris (2½ hr.) or Brussels (2¼ hr.) and London's Waterloo Station in South Bank. In London, make reservations for *Eurostar* at ☎ **0870/530-0003.** Visitors from all over the world can make advance train reservations at www.eurostar.com. Waterloo is a stop on the Underground's Northern Line. From here, you can easily reach the city by Tube. Buses and taxis are readily available just outside the station.

NATIONAL RAIL (☎ **0845/748-4950**; www.nationalrail.co.uk) trains connect just about every major city in the U.K. to one of London's major train stations (Charing Cross, Liverpool, Paddington, Victoria, King's Cross, Waterloo, and Euston), some of which also handle traffic arriving from various points in continental Europe. All major train stations in Central London have Underground stations and offer easy access to buses and taxis.

By Bus

Bus connections to Britain from the Continent, using the Channel Tunnel (Chunnel) or ferry services, are generally not very comfortable, so I can't recommend them. **NATIONAL EXPRESS** (☎ **0870/580-8080**; www.nationalexpress.com) buses traveling within the U.K. generally use centrally located Victoria Station as their terminus. The station, a few blocks from Buckingham Palace, is a stop on the Underground's District and Circle lines. It also has a taxi stand and is the terminus for many local city buses.

Getting **Around**

Discount Travel Passes

TRAVELCARDS offer unlimited use of buses, Underground, and British Rail services in Greater London, which makes them a good deal.

North American visitors can buy a **LONDON VISITOR TRAVELCARD** online through Rail Europe (www.raileurope.com). The card allows unlimited transport within Zones 1 and 2 of Greater London's Underground and bus network, as well as some discounts on London attractions. A 3-day pass costs $24 adults, $11 kids 5 to 15; a 7-day pass costs $36 adults, $15 kids 5 to 15. The Visitor Travelcard is a bit cheaper than the regular version, and you won't need to submit a photo to get a 7-day pass.

You can easily buy a regular daily, 3-day, or 7-day Travelcard at any Tube station. To get a 7-day Travelcard that covers all six of London's Public Transport zones, you'll also need to buy a Photocard ID and supply a passport-size photograph. Daily and 3-day Travelcards can be purchased at any Tube station ticket machine.

Discount public transport passes can be bought at any Underground station. They can be used on both the Tube and buses. The **1-DAY TRAVELCARD** costs £6 (£4.70 for weekday travel before 9:30am and on weekends and holidays) in Zones 1 and 2. Kids ages 5 to 15 pay £2. A **3-DAY TRAVELCARD** for Zones 1 and 2 costs £15 for adults and £7.50 for kids 5 to 15.

The **FAMILY TRAVELCARD** covers up to two adults and four children traveling together for a single day, with unlimited trips in Zones 1 and 2 (most of Central London), for £3.10 per adult and 80p per child; it costs £4 per adult and 80p per child for Zones 1 through 6. Children 5 to 15 travel free with this Travelcard on Saturday, Sunday, and public holidays.

OYSTER CARDS are pre-paid, re-usable "smart" cards that deduct the cost of a trip each time you touch your card to the yellow card-reader found on all public transportation (including the Docklands Light Railway and National Rail). The Oyster Card can be purchased at any Tube station or online. For more information, call ☎ **0870/849-9999** or check out www.oystercard.com.

You can also buy a discount **CAR-NET** booklet of 10 single Underground tickets valid only for Zones 1 and 2; you'll save about £3. A book of six single-journey **BUS SAVER** tickets can be bought at Tube stations for £6.

Surf the very comprehensive London Transport website at www.londontransport.co.uk for more information on discount options.

By Underground

The world's first underground train (known today as the Underground or Tube) was born in London in 1863. Stifling, overpopulated cars, sudden mysterious stops, and arbitrary line closures make the Underground the sacred monster of London's commuters (though visitors often adore it—I know New Yorkers who prefer it to the Big Apple's famous subways). Love it or loathe it, it's the lifeblood of the city, and its 12 lines (plus the Docklands Light Railway to Greenwich) are still the quickest way to get around the city.

All Tube stations are clearly marked with a red circle and blue crossbar. Routes are conveniently color-coded. The Tube runs daily, except Christmas, from 5:30am to

12:30am (until 11:30pm Sun), after which you must take a night bus or taxi. Fares start at £2 for a single journey within Zones 1 and 2 and climb to £3.80 for a one-way, all-Zone ticket. Buy your ticket or Travelcard from a machine inside the Tube station (some of them take credit cards) or from a clerk at a ticket window, insert it into the turnstile, and then retrieve it and hold onto it—it must be presented when you exit the station at your destination or you'll pay a fine.

Study a Tube map (obtainable at most major Underground stations) or consult the indispensable *London A to Z* street atlas (available at most London bookstores and newsstands) to find the stop nearest your destination. Note that you may have to switch lines in order to get from one destination to another. For more information on the Tube, check out www.londontransport.co.uk.

By Bus

The city's bus system is almost as good as the Underground, is comparably priced, and gives you better views of the city. Of course, you have to be prepared to be stuck in traffic. The city's red buses are almost a tourist attraction in their own right. Route maps are available at major Underground stations (Euston, Victoria, and Piccadilly Circus, to name a few). You can also call a 24-hour hot line (☎ **0207/222-1234**) for schedule and fare information.

Fares start at £1.20 for Zones 1 and 2, with prices rising the farther out you travel from Central London. Kids under 11 ride free, those ages 11 through 15 pay 40p, but a photo bus pass is required for the 14- and 15-year-olds. All Travelcards are valid on buses. Many Central London buses require that you buy your bus ticket from a ticket machine at a bus stop before boarding; these machines take exact change only. If there is no machine at your bus stop, you can pay the driver or conductor in cash (use small bills or coins only).

Double-decker buses are entered from the front. Pay the driver with cash, show your bus ticket, show your Travelcard, or touch your Oyster Card to the card-reader as you board.

Night buses are the only way to get around by public transport after the Tube stops operating. Be sure that there is an "N" bus listed on your bus stop's route or you'll wait in vain until morning.

By Taxi

All airport and train stations have well-marked areas for London's legendary black cabs, many of which are now colored with advertising, but are still the same distinctive model that holds five people. You can hail a taxi anywhere, on any street, except in certain no-stopping zones marked by white zigzag lines. Available taxis will have a lit sign on top of the cab. Taxis can also be requested by phone—the meter starts from the moment your cab is dispatched.

Only black cabs, whose drivers have undergone rigorous training known in England as "the Knowledge," are allowed to cruise the streets for fares. Don't get into cruising minicabs, which can legally pick up only those passengers who have booked them by telephone. Black cabs have metered fares (the flag drops at £3.80), and surcharges are assessed after 8pm and on weekends. Minicab charges should be negotiated in advance.

To book a black cab, call **RADIO TAXIS** (☎ **0207/272-0272**) or **DIAL-A-CAB** (☎ **0207/253-5000**). For a minicab, call **ADDISON LEE** (☎ **0207/387-8888**).

Fast **Facts**

APARTMENT RENTALS **Manors & Co.** (☎ 0207/486-5982; www.londonapartment.co.uk) offers serviced apartments in various locations throughout the city. **Home from Home** (☎ 0207/233-8111; www.homefromhome.co.uk) has a good website that displays all kinds of apartments in numerous London locations.

ATMS Called "Cashpoints" by the British, ATMs are everywhere, and most use global networks such as Cirrus and PLUS. Note that you may be charged a fee for withdrawing pounds from your foreign currency account.

BABYSITTING Reputable babysitting agencies with vetted employees include **Childminders** (☎ 0207/935-3000; www.babysitter.co.uk) and **Universal Aunts** (☎ 0207/738-8937). Rates run about £7 per hour during the day; £6 per hour in the evening. Hotel guests must pay a £10 booking fee and reasonable transportation costs.

BANKING HOURS Most banks are open Monday through Friday from 9am to 4:30pm.

B&BS **Bulldog Club,** 14 Dewhurst Rd. (☎ 0207/371-3202; www.bulldogclub.com); and **Uptown Reservations,** 8 Kelso Place (☎ 0207/351-3445; www.uptownres.co.uk), are two good reservation companies that offer lovely accommodations at bed-and-breakfasts in good neighborhoods.

BIKE RENTALS **London Bicycle Tour Company,** Gabriel's Wharf, South Bank (☎ 0207/928-6838; www.londonbicycle.com) rents a wide variety of bikes. Rates start at £2.50 per hour, and £14 per day.

BUSINESS HOURS Stores generally open at 10am and close around 6pm Monday through Saturday, though they may stay open until 7 or 8pm 1 night a week (usually Thurs). Some stores are open on Sunday from 11am or noon until 5pm. Post offices are open 9am to 5:30pm.

CLIMATE See "Weather," below.

CONCERTS See "Tickets," below.

CONSULATES AND EMBASSIES **American Embassy,** 24 Grosvenor Sq. (☎ 0207/499-9000; www.usembassy.org.uk). **Canadian High Commission,** 38 Grosvenor St. (☎ 0207/258-6600; www.canada.org.uk). **Australian High Commission,** Australia House, Strand (☎ 0207/379-4334; www.australia.org.uk). **Irish Embassy,** 17 Grosvenor Place (☎ 0207/235-7700). **New Zealand High Commission,** New Zealand House, 80 Haymarket (☎ 0207/930-8422; www.nzembassy.com).

CUSTOMS Check **www.hmce.gov.uk** for what foreign visitors may bring into London. For specifics on what you can bring home with you, Americans should consult the **U.S. Customs** website at www.customs.gov or call ☎ 202/354-1000. Canadians should contact the **Canadian Customs and Revenue Agency** (☎ 800/461-9999; www.ccra-adrc.gc.ca). Australians should contact **Australian Customs Services** (☎ 02/6275-6666; www.customs.gov.au). New Zealanders should contact **New Zealand Customs** (☎ 1800/428-786-60; www.customs.govt.nz).

DENTISTS **Dental Emergency Care Service,** Guy's Hospital (☎ 0207/955-2186), will guide you to a nearby dentist.

DINING Breakfasts range from the traditional meal of fried eggs, bacon, beans, grilled tomato, and toast, to a more continental menu of croissants, baguettes, and coffee. If your hotel doesn't include breakfast in its rates, breakfast in a cafe will likely be cheaper. Most cafes open from 8am to 8pm. Most restaurants open for lunch from noon to 3pm, and for dinner from 6 to 10 or 11pm. Dress codes have become much more relaxed, and except at very expensive restaurants and hotel dining rooms, no one will raise an eyebrow at casual clothing. You will encounter general disapproval if you bring small children to the nicer restaurants, especially at dinnertime.

Reservations at London's fanciest restaurants, such as The Ivy (p 102) sometimes require bookings of up to 2 months in advance. The same applies to the city's best luxe afternoon teas. Your best bet is to call the restaurant directly or reserve via its website. Many London restaurants take reservations via the Web through www.toptable. co.uk. You can also ask your hotel's concierge for help when you arrive in London or, better yet, at the time you reserve your room.

DOCTORS   A number of on-call doctor services can treat you and dispense medicine at your lodgings, or direct you to a walk-in clinic. Try **Doctor Direct** (☎ **0800/362-867;** www.doctorsdirect.co.uk); **Doctorcall** (☎ **0700/037-2255;** www. doctorcall.co.uk); and **Pharmacentre** (☎ **0808/108-5720;** www. pharmacentre.com).

ELECTRICITY   Britain uses a 220–240 volt system and alternating current (AC); its electrical plugs have three pins. European appliances will require only a plug adapter, but American 110-volt appliances will need both a transformer and adapter or they will fry and blow a fuse. Most laptops have built-in electrical transformers, but will need an adapter plug.

EMBASSIES   See "Consulates and Embassies," above.

EMERGENCIES   Call ☎ **999** for accidents and dire medical emergencies free of charge from any phone. Hospitals with emergency rooms (known as Accident and Emergency departments or A&E) in Central London include: **Charing Cross Hospital,** Fulham Palace Road, Hammersmith (☎ **0208/846-1234**); **Chelsea & Westminster Hospital,** Fulham Road, Chelsea (☎ **0208/746-8000**); **St. Mary's Hospital,** Praed Street, Paddington (☎ **0207/886-6666**); and **St. Thomas's Hospital,** Lambeth Palace Road, Lambeth (☎ **0207/928-9292**).

EVENT LISTINGS   Good sources of event and entertainment listings include *Time Out,* the "Metro" section of Thursday's *Evening Standard*, *What's On,* and the Saturday and Sunday supplements in London's daily newspapers.

FAMILY TRAVEL   Look for items tagged with a "kids" icon in this book. Most British hotels accommodate families; all but the poshest restaurants are usually family-friendly. The London Tourist Board operates a kid-friendly website, **Kids Love London** (www.kidslovelondon. com), that provides information on family-friendly attractions, events, restaurants, and more. For details, contact **Kidsline** (☎ **0207/487-5040**) or pick up a copy of *Frommer's London with Kids* (Wiley Publishing, Inc.) at your local bookstore.

GAY AND LESBIAN TRAVELERS   London has one of the most active lesbian and gay scenes in the world. The **London Lesbian & Gay Switchboard** (☎ **0207/837-7324;** www. llgs.org.uk) provides advice on everything from gay-friendly lodging to entertainment.

HEALTH CLUBS   Only expensive hotels have on-site health clubs, but many hotels have arrangements with nearby facilities that allow guests to use them. Many London health clubs offer day passes to the public for £15 to £50. Two good clubs with multiple London locations are **Holmes Place** (www.holmes place.co.uk) and **LA Fitness** (www.lafitness.co.uk).

HOLIDAYS Bank holidays, on which most shops and all banks, museums, public buildings, and services are closed, are as follows: New Year's Day, Good Friday (Fri before Easter); Easter Monday; May Day (first Mon in May); Spring Break (last Mon in May); Summer Break (last Mon in Aug); Christmas Day; and Boxing Day (Dec 26).

INSURANCE Check your existing insurance policies and credit card coverage before buying travel insurance. You may already be covered for lost luggage, canceled tickets, or medical expenses. If you aren't covered, expect to pay 5% to 8% of your trip's cost for insurance. For trip-cancellation and lost-luggage insurance, North Americans should try **Travel Guard International** (☎ **800/826-4919;** www.travel guard.com) or **Travel Insured International** (☎ **800/243-3174;** www.travelinsured.com). North Americans interested in getting medical insurance, including emergency evacuation coverage, can contact **Travel Assistance International** (☎ **800/821-2828;** www.travelassistance.com). U.K. travelers should contact **The Association of British Insurers** (☎ **020/7600-3333;** www.abi.org.uk), which gives advice by phone and publishes *Holiday Insurance,* a free guide to policy provisions and prices. You might also shop around for better deals: Try **Columbus Direct** (☎ **020/7375-0011;** www.columbusdirect.net).

INTERNET CAFES Most major streets have cybercafes. **EasyEverything** (www.easyeverything.co.uk), a popular chain of Internet cafes, offers cheap, around-the-clock Web access. It has 20 London branches, including

ones in Trafalgar Square and Piccadilly Circus.

LOST PROPERTY Be sure to tell all your credit card companies the minute you discover your wallet has been lost or stolen, and file a report at the nearest police precinct (your insurance company may require a police report before covering any claims). If you've lost all forms of photo ID, call your consulate and airline and explain the situation. It's always best to keep copies of your credit card numbers and passport information in a separate location in case you lose the real items.

For help in finding lost property, call **British Rail** (☎ **0870/000-5151**); **London Underground** (☎ **0207/918-2000**); **London Transport buses** (☎ **0207/222-1234**); or black cabs (☎ **0207/918-2000**).

MAIL AND POSTAGE Stamps for mail inside the European Union cost 28p for first class and 20p for second class. Postage for postcards sent outside the E.U. cost 42p; letters cost 68p. Most newsagents carry stamps, and the city's distinctive red mailboxes are plentiful. The main post office in Trafalgar Square has the longest hours in London: 8:30am to 6:30pm Monday to Friday, and 9am to 5:30pm Saturday.

MONEY England clings stubbornly to its pound sterling and pence. £1 consists of 100 pence (pennies). There are one- and two-pound coins; silvery 50p, 20p, 10p, and 5p coins; and copper 2p and 1p coins. Bank notes are issued in denominations of £50 (red), £20 (lavender), £10 (orange), and £5 (blue).

Foreign money can be exchanged at most banks and *bureaux de change,* but you'll be assessed a hefty surcharge or get terrible conversion rates. If you want to arrive with a few pounds in hand, get them from your bank before you leave home. ATMs (called Cashpoints) are located all over the city and offer the best exchange rates; find out your daily withdrawal limit before you leave home. At this writing, £1 was worth a hefty $1.86. For the most up-to-date currency conversion information, go to www.xe.com.

Many stores in London will not take traveler's checks, and those that do often charge stiff fees. It's best to stick to cash and credit cards, though most banks assess a 2% fee above the 1% fee charged by Visa, MasterCard, or American Express for currency conversions. Be sure to notify your credit card companies before leaving for London, so they don't get become suspicious when the card is used numerous times in London and block your charges.

PARKING Parking in London is difficult even for those who have paid for a resident parking permit (yet another reason I advise against renting a car here). Metered spaces have time limits of 1 to 4 hours and are hard to find.

Garages (car parks) are expensive, but plentiful. Look for signs that say **ncp** (for National Car Park); call ☎ **0207/499-7050** or check out www.ncp.co.uk for locations and more information.

Always check any yellow warning signs on streets for info on temporary parking suspensions. Parking violations are punished with a hefty fine, tire clamping, or the removal of your car to an impound lot. If your car has been towed, call ☎ **0207/747-7474**.

PASSES London's biggest museums are free now, but the comprehensive **London Pass** (www.londonpass.com) offers more than enough discounts and benefits to make it worth buying. The pass includes a free Travelcard (see "Getting Around" on p 157) covering Zones 1 through 6, discounts at theaters and restaurants, guided museum tours, and free entry to over 50 attractions and special exhibitions that charge admission, such as the various royal palaces, the London Aquarium, and the Globe Theatre. Prices range from £27 for adults (£17 for kids) for a 1-day pass, to £94 for adults (£52 for kids) for a 6-day pass.

PASSPORTS Citizens of the United States, Canada, Ireland, Australia, and New Zealand need only a valid passport to enter England. **U.S. residents** can download passport applications from the U.S. State Department website at http://travel.state.gov/passport_services.html. Passport applications for **Canadian citizens** are available at local travel agencies and through the Passport Office, Department of Foreign Affairs and International Trade, Ottawa, ON K1A 0G3 (☎ **800/567-6868;** www.ppt.gc.ca). **Irish residents** can apply for a 10-year passport at the Passport Office, Setanta Centre, Molesworth Street, Dublin 2 (☎ **01/671-1633;** www.irlgov.ie/iveagh). **Australians** should contact the Australian Passport Information Service at ☎ **131-232,** or visit the government website at www.passports.gov.au. **New Zealand residents** can download applications from the Passports Office's website at www.passports.govt.nz.

Always make a copy of your passport's information page and keep it separate from your passport in case of loss or theft. For emergency passport replacement, contact your country's embassy or consulate (see "Consulates and Embassies," on p 159).

PHARMACIES These "chemists" can fill a valid doctor's prescription from home. One late-night pharmacy (open until midnight) is **Bliss Chemist,** 5–6 Marble Arch (☎ **0207/723-6116**). The leading drugstore chain in the U.K., **Boots the Chemist** (www.boots.com), has branches all over London.

SAFETY London has its share of violent crime, just as any other major city does—its biggest crime-related problems are muggings and rape—but it is much safer than most cities its size, and is usually quite safe for visitors so long as you take common-sense precautions. Good safety tips include:

- Use your hotel safe.

- Be alert when withdrawing money from ATMs; don't take out more cash than you need, and don't carry large sums around.

- Guard your valuables in public places and keep your wallet in an inner pocket. Pickpockets operate in all the major tourist zones.

- Don't leave pocketbooks dangling from chairs in restaurants; use a purse that closes securely.

- Avoid conspicuous displays of expensive jewelry.

- Avoid the upper decks of buses late at night. Take a cab if you can afford it.

- Stay alert in high-end shopping areas: Bags from luxury shops are a tip-off to thieves.

- There's safety in numbers—don't wander alone in Soho or the West End late at night. And stay out of parks after dark.

- Don't hop in a minicab hailed off the street. Stick to official black cabs.

- Women dressed in ethnic Gypsy clothes, holding strangely quiet children, are part of a well-organized and creepy gang of rip-off artists similar to the Gypsy thieves that plague Rome and Paris. Don't approach them.

SENIOR TRAVELERS Discounts (concessions) for seniors over 64 are available (with proof of age) for museums, public transport, and entertainment. **Elderhostel** (☎ 877/426-8056; www.elderhostel.org) organizes well-priced "study trips" to many world destinations, including London; the courses are geared toward active seniors, and accommodations may be spartan.

SMOKING Smoking is prohibited in shops, on all public transportation, and inside Tube stations. Most restaurants have a nonsmoking section, but bars and pubs are often free-for-alls. If you smoke, tobacco is expensive in the U.K., so bring your cigarettes from home or buy them in the airport duty-free shop.

SPECTATOR SPORTS London is crazy for football (that's soccer to you Americans out there) and is home to three professional teams. The best place to watch the English lose their decorum in the stands is the Chelsea Club, Stanford Bridge, Fulham Road (☎ **0207/386-7799;** www.chelseafc.co.uk). Wear blue and you'll fit right in. For a more genteel (albeit confusing) experience, try watching a cricket match at the sport's most hallowed field—Lords Cricket Club, St. John's Wood Road (☎ **0207/432-1066;** www.lords.org.uk).

The most sacred annual London sporting event is June's Lawn Tennis Championships at Wimbledon (☎ **0208/971-2473;** www.wimbledon.com). If you want to down strawberries and cream on Centre Court, you'll need to enter a January ticket lottery first—call or check the website for details. Same-day seats to the outside courts are available, but you'll wait in very long lines.

TAXES A 17.5% value-added tax (VAT) is assessed on hotel and restaurant bills, merchandise, and most services. Non-E.U. visitors are eligible for partial VAT refunds (for more information, see p 84). Note that price tags on items in stores already include the VAT. Gasoline (petrol) in Britain is taxed at 25%.

TAXIS See "By Taxi," on p 158.

TELEPHONES London has three types of public pay phones: those accepting only coins, those accepting only phone cards (Cardphones), and those that take both phone cards and most major credit cards. Phone cards can be purchased in several denominations (£2–£20) at most newsstands and post offices. The minimum charge for a local call is 10p.

London's city code is 020, but you don't need to dial it within city limits; just dial the eight-digit number. To call London from the rest of the U.K., you must dial the 020 followed by the number. When calling London from abroad, dial the international code (011 from North America; 0011 from Australia; and 00 from New Zealand), followed by 44 (England's country code), followed by 20, and then the eight-digit number.

When calling abroad from London, dial 00, the country code, the area code, and then the number. Directory assistance in London can be reached by calling ☎ **118 180**, but try to dial numbers direct, because connection costs through directory assistance companies are high.

TICKETS Most West End theaters keep a few seats in reserve to sell on the day of a performance. If you're set on seeing a specific show or event (especially the ballet or opera), book your tickets in advance (for a small service fee) through **Londontown** (www.londowntown.com), **Ticketmaster** (www.ticketmaster. co.uk), **Albemarle** (www.Albemarle-London.com), or **Keith Prowse** (www.keithprowse.com). You can also try calling the box office directly.

You can get half-price theater tickets at the free-standing kiosk on the south side of Leicester Square for same-day performances of selected shows. For more information on buying tickets in advance, see p 133.

TIPPING Check restaurant bills for an automatic service charge, which usually runs around 12% to 15%. If service hasn't been included, tip your waiter 15%. Tip taxi drivers, hairdressers, and bartenders 10% to 15%. It is not usual to tip hotel chambermaids, though you may certainly do so. Hotel porters should get £1 per bag; doormen should get £1 for hailing you a cab. You aren't expected to tip at a pub unless table service is provided.

TOILETS Clean, city-maintained public toilets can be found in shopping areas, parks, and tourist zones. Some charge 20p for use. Pubs and hotels don't get too fussy if you discreetly nip in to use the loo (especially if you buy a drink first). Department stores have public restrooms, but these are stashed on high floors to discourage traffic. For more information on public restrooms, see p 63.

TOURIST OFFICES Drop into the official **London Tourist Board Visitor Centre,** 1 Lower Regent St. (☎ **0207/808-3800;** www.visit london.com; Tube: Piccadilly Circus), for information in eight languages, useful pamphlets, maps, Travelcards, and souvenirs. The center also has a decent cafe and offers currency exchange and Internet access. It's open 9am to 6:30pm weekdays, and 10am to 4pm weekends.

TOURIST TRAPS AND SCAMS
Madame Tussaud's Wax Museum is London's most puzzlingly popular tourist trap—it's crowded, it's outrageously expensive, and it offers little cultural value. The half-price theater-ticket shops around Soho are rip-offs (they tag on a heavy commission for poor seats), and most tickets sold on the street are counterfeit; use only the official half-price ticket booth at the south end of Leicester Square. Forget the street peddlers selling perfume and accessories. See "Safety," above.

TOURS   Two similar companies offer good orientation tours of the city from the vantage of a double-decker bus: **London Big Bus** (☎ **0800/ 169-1365**; www.bigbus.co.uk); and **Original London Sightseeing Tour** (☎ **0208/877-1722**; www.the originaltour.com). Tickets, good for 24 hours, allow visitors to hop on and off buses that stop at most of Central London's major attractions (buses run every 15–30 min.). Both companies' tours take about 2 hours; audio commentary is available in a number of languages. The Big Bus tour ticket also covers a small selection of themed walking tours.

Black Taxi Tours of London (☎ **0207/935-9363**; www.blacktaxi tours.co.uk) offers personalized 2-hour tours in a genuine black cab for up to five people for £75. The cabs can venture where buses cannot, making it easier to get off the tourist trail.

For walking tours of London that are geared to particular interests or themes, you can't do better than **The Original London Walks** (☎ **0207/624-3978**; www.walks. com). Expert guides lead visitors on tours ranging from ghost walks to strolls through literary London to historic pub crawls.

If you want to tour London via the Thames, **City Cruises** (☎ **0207/ 740-0400**; www.citycruises.com) offers sightseeing trips in modern river boats equipped with audio commentary in six languages. Tours depart from Westminster, Waterloo, and Tower piers; they range in duration from 30 minutes to 2½ hours.

Many of the city's museums and royal palaces offer daily gallery talks and themed tours inspired by the various objects in their collections. TRAVELERS WITH DISABILITIES   Most of London's major museums are fitted with wheelchair ramps. Discounts for travelers with disabilities, known as "concessions," are offered by many attractions and theaters. **Holiday Care Services** (☎ **0845/ 124-9971** in the U.K.; 0208/760-0072 outside the U.K.; www.holiday care.org.uk) offers loads of information and advice for travelers with disabilities visiting Britain. The **Greater London Action on Disability** (☎ **0207/346-5800**; www.glad.org.uk) gives advice on accessibility to London visitors. Visitors with disabilities planning to travel via public transportation should order *Access to the Underground,* a helpful pamphlet put out by **London Transport** (☎ **0207/ 222-1235**; www.londontransport. co.uk).

VAT   See "Taxes," above.

WEATHER   For the local London forecast, call ☎ **0906/823-2771**; or go to http://uk.weather.com/ index.html for up-to-date weather information.

A Brief **History**

A.D. 43   Romans invade England and settle Londinium.

A.D. 61   Queen Boadicea sacks Londinium in a brutal but unsuccessful rebellion against Rome.

200   Romans fortify the city with a wall.

400   Roman troops abandon London as the Empire falls.

600   King Ethelbert builds first St. Paul's Church on ruins of Temple of Diana.

800   Vikings raid Britain.

885   Alfred the Great captures London from the Vikings.

1042   Edward the Confessor is crowned king of England and begins work on Westminster Abbey.

1066   William the Conqueror is crowned king of England in Westminster Abbey after the Battle of Hastings. London becomes seat of political power.

1078   Construction of the Tower of London begins.

1176–1209   London Bridge is built, connecting the two banks of the Thames.

1192   Henry FitzAilwin is elected first lord mayor of London.

1215   Magna Carta is signed by King John.

1240   First Parliament is convened at Westminster.

1348   First outbreak of the Black Death plagues London.

1381   Wat Tyler's Peasant Revolt is mercilessly crushed.

1476   William Caxton, the first English printer, revolutionizes London and makes Fleet Street the country's publishing center.

1509   Henry VIII ascends the throne.

1534–36   Henry VIII breaks with Rome and establishes the Church of England, an action leading to the Dissolution of the Monasteries.

1553–58   Catholic Queen Mary I executes thousands of Protestants, earning the nickname "Bloody Mary."

1558   Elizabeth I is crowned.

1588   Spanish Armada defeated.

1599   Shakespeare's first play is performed at the Globe Theatre.

1605   Guy Fawkes' November 5 Gunpowder Plot to destroy Parliament is thwarted.

1642–58   English Civil War pits Royalists against Parliamentarians.

1649   Charles I is beheaded at Whitehall.

1653   Oliver Cromwell is made Lord Protector of the Realm. Puritan rule closes London's theaters, brothels, and gaming halls.

1660   Charles II is brought back from exile in France and the monarchy is restored.

1665   Outbreak of bubonic plague kills 100,000 Londoners.

1666   Great Fire of London sweeps through the city.

1667   Christopher Wren begins work on St. Paul's Cathedral; attempts to redraw London's map are abandoned.

1688 James II is banished during the Bloodless Revolution; William and Mary move into Kensington Palace.

1694 First Bank of England is established.

1735 Dr. Samuel Johnson moves to London and becomes a fixture on the coffeehouse circuit.

1759 The British Museum is opened to the public.

1829 Robert Peel sets up Metropolitan Police force, known as "bobbies" in his honor.

1836 Charles Dickens publishes *The Pickwick Papers* and becomes London's favorite novelist.

1837 Eighteen-year-old Queen Victoria ascends the throne and moves into Buckingham Palace.

1851 Great Exhibition takes place in Hyde Park, financing the development of South Kensington.

1854 Cholera epidemic in London results in improved sewage system.

1857 Victoria and Albert Museum opens.

1860 London's first public flushing toilet opens.

1863 London opens the world's first Underground Transit System.

1901 Queen Victoria dies; Edward VI is crowned.

1914 World War I starts; zeppelins drop bombs on London.

1936 King Edward VIII abdicates throne to marry American divorcée Wallis Simpson.

1939–45 World War II air raids kill thousands in London and destroy much of the city's infrastructure.

1953 Queen Elizabeth II is crowned.

1963 Youth-quake in London: The Beatles and the Rolling Stones rule the day.

1970s Irish Republican Army engages in terrorist bomb offensive.

1979 Margaret Thatcher becomes England's first female prime minister.

1981 Prince Charles marries Lady Diana Spencer in St. Paul's Cathedral.

1994 Channel Tunnel opens.

1997 Tony Blair becomes prime minister of England; London mourns the death of Princess Diana.

2000 Traditional pigeon-feeding in Trafalgar Square is outlawed.

2002 London celebrates Elizabeth II's Golden Jubilee.

2004 A London warehouse fire destroys British modern art worth £50 million.

London's **Architecture**

Norman Period: 1066–1200

The oldest surviving style of architecture in London dates back to the time of William the Conqueror, when the Normans overran England. Thick walls and masonry were used to support the large interiors needed to accommodate the church-going masses. The heavy construction usually gave Norman buildings a dark and foreboding air.

Characteristics of the period include:

- Thick walls with small windows
- Round weight-bearing arches
- Huge piers (square stacks of masonry)
- Chevrons—zigzagging decorations surrounding doorways or wrapped around columns.

The Tower of London's **WHITE TOWER,** built by William the Conqueror, is a textbook example of a Norman-style castle. **ST. JOHN'S CHAPEL** within the White Tower is one of the few remaining Norman-style churches in England.

Gothic: 1150–1550

French in origin, the fairy-tale Gothic style introduced innovations that allowed builders to transfer weight away from a structure's walls, so they could be taller and thinner. The style also allowed for the use of larger windows, which allowed more natural light to reach a building's interior.

In addition to the pointed arch, Gothic construction features:

- Vaulted ceilings, using cross vaulting (an "X" design) and fan vaulting (a more conic design)
- Flying buttresses, free-standing exterior pillars that helped support the buildings' weight

White Tower

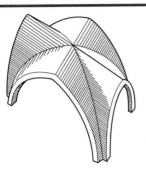

Cross Vault

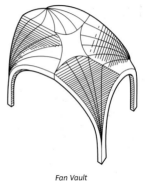

Fan Vault

- Carved tracery stonework connecting windows
- Stained-glass windows.

You need look no further than **WEST-MINSTER ABBEY,** built in the mid–14th century, for a perfect London example of the Gothic style.

Renaissance: 1550–1650

The Renaissance style, involving proportion and mathematical precision enlivened by decoration, was imported from the Continent by the great Inigo Jones, who was greatly influenced by Italian Palladianism.

Characteristics of Renaissance architecture include:

- A sense of proportion
- A reliance on symmetry

- The use of classical columns—Doric, Ionic, and Corinthian.

Top examples of this style include the **BANQUETING HALL AT WHITE-HALL** and the **ARCADE** of Covent Garden, both designed by Inigo Jones.

Baroque: 1650–1750

Baroque architects Christopher Wren and Nicholas Hawksmoor had unrivalled opportunities to practice their craft in London when the Great Fire of 1666 provided a clean palette on which to replace medieval wooden structures.

The prime features of the more fanciful baroque style include:

- Classical forms marked by grand curving lines
- Decoration with playful carvings.

Classical Orders

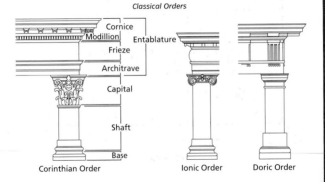

Corinthian Order — Ionic Order — Doric Order

Cornice, Modillion, Entablature, Frieze, Architrave, Capital, Shaft, Base

ST. PAUL'S CATHEDRAL, with its massive dome and complex exterior decor, is Wren's crowning achievement and the finest example of English baroque architecture in London.

Neoclassical and Greek Revival: 1714–1837

Neoclassicism was an 18th-century reaction to the busy nature of baroque architecture. Notable characteristics of neoclassical architecture include:

- Clean, elegant lines, with balance and symmetry
- Use of classical Greek columns
- Crescent layouts (half-circles of identical stone houses with tall windows).

SIR JOHN SOANE'S MUSEUM, and John Nash's curving white stucco **CUMBERLAND TERRACE** in Regent's Park, are exemplars of these styles.

Victorian Gothic Revival: 1750–1900

As industrialism began its inexorable march on London, artists and architects looked back to a simpler and more romantic fairy-tale period for their inspiration.

The features that marked the Gothic Revival style include:

- A confusion of spires, arches, and decorative detail
- Buildings constructed on a grand scale.

St. Paul's Cathedral

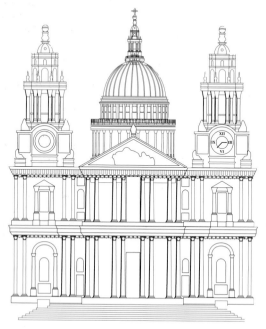

Palace of Westminster

The **PALACE OF WESTMINSTER,** home to the British Parliament, is the farthest-reaching exponent of this style; the most compact is the Albert Memorial in Hyde Park.

20th and Early 21st Century: 1900–present

The 20th century saw London expanding into its suburbs with uninspired architecture. The Blitz was the period's (far more tragic) version of the Great Fire, and rebuilding took place with post-war austerity.

The ugly, utilitarian style of South Bank's Royal Festival Hall is known as **BRUTALISM. POST-MODERNISM** is a softening of that style, applying the whimsy of the past to the modern, which brought about the inside-out **LLOYD'S BUILDING,** and the **GHERKIN BUILDING.** The best marriage of old and new can be seen in the covered **GREAT COURT** of the British Museum, which managed to put a new hat on an old friend without making it look silly.

The Wren Style

One of the great geniuses of his age (and London's greatest architect), Sir Christopher Wren (1632–1723) was a professor of astronomy at Oxford before becoming an architect. After the Great Fire of London in 1666, Wren was chosen to rebuild the devastated city and its many churches, including St. Paul's, on which work began in 1675. His designs had great originality, and he became known for his spatial effects and his impressive fusion of classical and baroque. He believed in classical stability and repose, yet he liked to enliven his churches with baroque whimsy and fantasy. Nothing better represents the Wren style than the facade of St. Paul's (p. 13, bullet ⓫), for which he combined classical columns, reminiscent of Greek temples, with baroque decorations and adornments.

2

Toll-free Numbers and Websites

Airlines

AER LINGUS
☎ 800/474-7424 in the U.S.
☎ 01/886-8888 in Ireland
www.aerlingus.com

AIR CANADA
☎ 888/247-2262
www.aircanada.ca

AIR NEW ZEALAND
☎ 0800/737-767 in New Zealand
www.airnewzealand.com

AMERICAN AIRLINES
☎ 800/433-7300
www.aa.com

BRITISH AIRWAYS
☎ 800/247-9297
☎ 0845/77-333-77 in Britain
www.british-airways.com

CONTINENTAL AIRLINES
☎ 800/525-0280
www.continental.com

DELTA AIR LINES
☎ 800/221-1212
www.delta.com

EASYJET
No number.
www.easyjet.com

NORTHWEST AIRLINES
☎ 800/225-2525
www.nwa.com

QANTAS
☎ 800/227-4500 in the U.S.
☎ 13 13 13 in Australia
www.qantas.com

RYANAIR
☎ 0818 30 30 30 in Ireland
☎ 0871/246-0000 in the U.K.
☎ 01 353 1 249 7700 for the U.S.
www.ryanair.com

UNITED AIRLINES
☎ 800/241-6522
www.united.com

US AIRWAYS
☎ 800/428-4322
www.usairways.com

VIRGIN ATLANTIC AIRWAYS
☎ 800/862-8621 in the U.S.
☎ 0870/380-2007 in Britain
www.virgin-atlantic.com

Car Rental Agencies

ALAMO
☎ 800/327-9633
www.goalamo.com

AUTO EUROPE
☎ 800/223-5555
www.autoeurope.com

AVIS
☎ 800/331-1212 in the U.S.
☎ 800/TRY-AVIS in Canada
www.avis.com

BUDGET
☎ 800/527-0700
www.budget.com

DOLLAR
☎ 800/800-4000
www.dollar.com

ENTERPRISE
☎ 800/325-8007
www.enterprise.com

HERTZ
☎ 800/654-3131
www.hertz.com

KEMWEL HOLIDAY AUTO
☎ 800/678-0678 or 877/820-0668
www.kemwel.com

NATIONAL
☎ 800/CAR-RENT
www.nationalcar.com

THRIFTY
☎ 800/367-2277
www.thrifty.com

Major Hotel and Motel Chains

BEST WESTERN INTERNATIONAL
☎ 800/528-1234
www.bestwestern.com

COMFORT INNS
☎ 800/228-5150
www.hotelchoice.com

CROWNE PLAZA HOTELS
☎ 888/303-1746
www.crowneplaza.com

DAYS INN
☎ 800/325-2525
www.daysinn.com

HILTON HOTELS
☎ 800/HILTONS
www.hilton.com

HOLIDAY INN
☎ 800/HOLIDAY
www.ichotelsgroup.com

HYATT HOTELS & RESORTS
☎ 800/228-9000
www.hyatt.com

INTER-CONTINENTAL HOTELS & RESORTS
☎ 888/567-8725
www.ichotelsgroup.com

RADISSON HOTELS INTERNATIONAL
☎ 800/333-3333
www.radisson.com

RED CARNATION HOTELS
☎ 877/955-1515
www.redcarnation hotels.com

SHERATON HOTELS & RESORTS
☎ 800/325-3535
www.sheraton.com

THISTLE HOTELS
☎ 0870/333-9292
www.thistlehotels.com

Index

Photo **Credits**

p ii, top: © Chris Ladd/Getty Images; p ii, 3rd from top: © Ellen Rooney/Robert Harding World Imagery/Getty Images; p ii, 4th from top: © Jeremy Horner/Corbis; p ii, 5th from top: © Richard I'Anson/Lonely Planet Images; p iii, 4th from top: Neil Setchfield/Lonely Planet Images; p iii, 5th from top: © courtesy The Savoy; p viii@@hyp 1: © Mark Polott/Index Stock

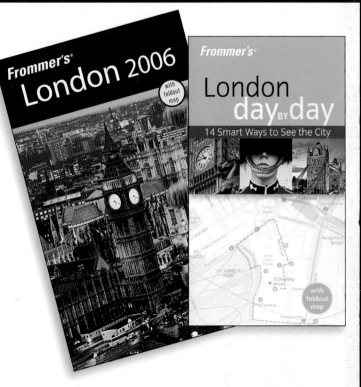